WOKE & PROUD

The Charlatans' Inconvenience

WOKE & PROUD

The Charlatans' Inconvenience

J. Marcelo Baqueroalvarez

WARNING: *Read this book only if you* <u>truly</u> *have an open mind, if not... you are still welcome to buy it and have it readily available for whenever you mind opens up. This book will be waiting for you. This book will challenge you, pull you in all directions, and augment the way you see the world today – yes, seriously.*

Are you ready?

WOKE & PROUD
| The Charlatans' Inconvenience

Published via BeeZee Vision, LLC.™, Chesapeake, Virginia, USA,
in collaboration with Half Life Crisis™, Chesapeake, Virginia, USA.

Paperback ISBN: 979-8-9893753-2-5
E-Book ISBN: 979-8-9893753-3-2

HLC Control Number: 23-0300023-M

For my wife Alicia and daughter Samantha.
I don't know how far my words will travel, but I am well aware that no matter where I am I will always love you.

WOKE & PROUD

The Charlatans' Inconvenience

CONTENTS

FOREWORD

A few years ago when you heard the term "WOKE" was almost a compliment. Fast forward to when I am typing this manuscript, and this term has been transformed akin to a derogatory epithet. Or is it? The short answer is: "It depends." The long answer? This entire book. The term has been hijacked by many figures on particular platforms which find "woke" people inconvenient.

And this term, or the concept behind is nothing relatively new. However, it has lately taken a lot more political baggage because of the evolving geo-political situation around the world. I also wrote a book which deals with authoritarianism and propaganda; and people who might be falling under this "woke" category could very well be considered archnemeses to propagandists. However, there are also those who are just confused and yelling platitudes to the world. And startling enough, many confused people do get a cult following regardless if their assertions are spot on, or are indeed platitudes.

Every time I keep hearing politicians or media talking-heads demonizing the term "woke," it seems that their definition keeps morphing. Unsurprisingly, this morphing also seems to occur from those defending "woke" in today's society. In the United States of America, there have even been politicians who set-forth bills and possibly getting legislation passed to combat what some call "*wokism*" when referring to the "woke" people in this country.

The topic for this book has been tumbling in my head for several weeks now, even though I have been familiar with the term for several years. Finally today, Friday, March 17, 2023 just a couple of hours before midnight I finally get a chance to start this manuscript. As with other books I've written, I am typing this in my bunk at the end of the work-day onboard the world-famous USS COLE DDG-67. We are underway, we have been underway for a while, and we have a lot more time left out to sea. That gives me a chance to use any down-time I can afford for a better use… as I put my thoughts into words.

Because of the volatility of this topic, I will not be taking any sides for or against "woke" – but rather try to bridge the gap. Also, the conceptualization for this term will be my interpretation based on historical trends, and an understanding of what being "woke" could mean to different segments of the population. Especially to groups in a position of power or expanded influence. I am not asking any readers to agree or disagree with my analysis. But I do hope my words will resonate with you because I write this with outmost objectivity. And yes, that might not make a few people happy. But facts are impervious to emotions. I will stick to the facts, and add my analysis based upon those facts.

Yes, we will explore facts. There will be zero emotional baggage coming from me. To be honest, I personally do not care one way or the other if somebody would designate me as "woke" or "non-woke" – I am who I am regardless. But I will be drawing parallels to the baggage associated with this term. Also, I will differentiate this concept from those who highjack the term for their own benefit, either for or against "woke" people. Normally I would have not really even cared too much about the general discord on this term, but in the last several months laws and other restrictions are being built around this paradigm. *That* I find concerning, because it could skew the general public's perception of reality.

Being "woke" against somebody put in charge could be inconvenient for that person in power. Is this bad or good? Think about it for a moment. What side of the equation are you for or against? Of course the very first chapter will address this question in detail. Later, in the book we will also talk about projection. In other words, are we guilty of the same flaws we fault others, when in reality we are displaying these very faults ourselves? How "woke" is too "woke?" Is there even such a thing, or is it a misconception based on a propagandistic means to an end?

I worry about these types of questions because I am an avid historian. And I've seen how parroting some terms and banalities could galvanize confused people to turn a dangerous rhetoric into action. As the geopolitical climate in the world becomes more and more volatile, I (as a functioning adult) owe it to the next generation to articulate in the best way possible what I see as an indicator for potential manipulation. Yes, in an effort to mitigate the next generation from being manipulated.

This book is intended to be relatively short. And there is a reason for it. Because I want this information to be available to you as soon as possible, and serve as a basis to enact critical thinking and intellectual honesty. If you are familiar with any of my other books and my writing, I am very big on that – critical thinking & intellectual honesty. Why? Because the more we understand our surroundings, the better this world will become for <u>all</u> of us.

We'll realize that we are a lot more similar than dissimilar. But that reality is not convenient for those who want to divide us Those who want to divide us need those artificial barriers in order to exercise their power over all of us. This is nothing new, but when you are aware of the situation, then your chances of being manipulated decrease dramatically. That knowledge you'll gain is not convenient for those who want to manipulate you. You'll hear a lot about that in this book. There is a reason why I emphasize it repeatedly.

Turning a blind eye is tacit consent for somebody else to control your life. Now *that* is something I do care about, a lot actually. Why? Because it affects the perception from other people in our society and it could turn a dystopian rhetoric into violent action. I am not even exaggerating. This is historically accurate. People who buy into a false narrative tend to exude violent outburst with perceived impunity. Especially if the rhetoric is giving them credence and "authorizing" them to act in a manner that could harm others.

For example, did you know that most of the authoritarians were able to galvanize their power because they lied to their followers? Yes, furthermore if they would have told them the [actual] truth, most people would have preferred not to follow them. In fact, many times when the followers realized they were bamboozled, they turned against the very dear leader they would have otherwise given their very lives for... just moments beforehand finding out that their dear leader actually betrayed them.

I wrote an entire book about that topic regarding authoritarians and their tactics. It is titled **Authoritarianism & Propaganda | The Puppet Master Tools**. In that book I talk in-depth about what I am speaking about in the previous paragraphs. And yes, these topics correlate because they are one of the many tools utilized by authoritarian propagandists. That is why I wrote this book to go along with that one.

We have to understand that many segments in our lives are linked directly or indirectly. The world functions in an abstract realm. Those who try to see it in a 100% concrete manner will always be vulnerable to exploitation. It is unfortunate, but it is true. And the fact is that these techniques have been exploited for centuries if not millennia. They work, and it is part of our human rationality.

The rationality can be highjacked based on our environment. What it is or it is not acceptable is a very subjective matter. Quick example, is it socially acceptable to be walking around with a loin cloth in a touristic-beach resort? Is it acceptable to wear a G-string thong in a similar situation? They both serve essentially the same function. The "design" might differ, but they essentially conceal just as much from one design to the other. Yes, I chose that example on purpose because I am sure that will get the imagination rolling.

This book will have a lot of examples about that. Not necessarily about loin cloths, but rather about what is and it is not acceptable in a particular society based on certain artificially mandated parameters. And guess what? Throughout history these levels of acceptability have morphed and changed. Want another example? Sure, why not?

The palace of Versailles, in France. Before the French Revolution, monarchs and people from the court's high society resided in this palace full of exuberant beauty and art. But there were no reliable bathrooms, and many nobles would just leave their human excrement and urine all over the place. And although disgusting, it was something pretty much normalized circa that time. Do that human excrement dropping today in the palace of Versailles and see how well it goes for you. *(Author's note – Please do not leave human excrement or urine outside the actual restrooms. And by that, I mean, instead leave all these human-fluids and potatoes inside the actual receptacles specifically designed to handle that type of waste – sorry, got to say that).* And the fact that I have to caveat this situation is another reason why I am writing this book.

Woke and *unreasonable* are two different things. People can be vulnerable or go to extremes. There are those who in their mind think they are *so woke* that they end up advocating or pushing for agendas that are incredibly shortsighted and petulant in nature. There is nothing wrong with trying to make things better for all people, and ensuring there are checks and balances. But there are parameters that should reside in reality, and not in a "utopian fantasy" that is divorced from common sense and truth.

In fact, some of those so called "woke" in a misappropriated sense of the word are actually advocating from unrealistic parameters that make it harder for the real "woke" to point some actual arguments that should warrant a second look and course correction. Again, these remarks might seem very abstract to the casual observer. That is why critical thinking and intellectual honesty are so important. In the following chapters we are going to dissect each one of these in a way that will help us reconcile reality with fairness and ultimately come up with better solutions.

The world will continue moving regardless if humans destroy the planet or not. The planet will eventually heal, but we will not be here to enjoy it anymore. That is why this topic needs to be addressed and understood. How "woke" is that?

INTRODUCTION

Hello, and thank you so much for reading my book!
Whatever the reason which brings you to read these words today, I am grateful because we will be discussing about a very misunderstood topic that seems to be taking a lot of traction. I have been hearing this "woke" terminology for so many months in ways that seem eerily demonized by particular segments of the world's population. And many of those who embrace as something good do not seem to understand it either. It seems that the definition keeps morphing and the goal post for what it is supposed to entitle keeps shifting over and over again. You would think the term has become a semantic scape goat to confuse the less informed segments of the population. I know, right?

As I type this, I am currently floating onboard the world-famous USS COLE DDG 67, we finished a few training evolutions in the Atlantic. They went very well by the way. We have a lot of additional time to be floating around, and we have been gone for a while. However, every now and then I get a few moments to myself. As we all should, not because Sailors are underway means that they are supposed to be slaves to the grind. All work and no rest would make any mission unsustainable. Sailors are people, and people are complex.

Under naval doctrine we are supposed to learn from any potential shortcomings we have, and we use these lessons learned to make ourselves better. And spoiler alert, we enact lessons learned even if everything went well, but we could be better. If there is something that is not going well, or somebody made a mistake, we will hold them accountable. If everybody is doing well, and it is working correctly, then we will continue enacting that course of action until something else gets identified that can make whatever we are doing better. Sounds reasonable enough, right?

Well, spoiler alert, being "woke" in the proper context is the very same thing! If it is working well, it gets assessed if it can be better, because everything needs to continue evolving, otherwise we will stagnate. If something is obviously wrong, or we've been able to get away with something that is wrong but it could potentially create harm in the future, then it needs to be addressed. These are called checks and balances. And yes, these are part of our innovative process.

Doing something forever, because it works fine and "it is the way it has always been" is ultimately counterproductive. Let me give you a quick example. Landline telephones back in the day worked very well when we used rotary phones (the old school telephones who had a spinning wheel with numbers to dial). I know that for a fact, because we had a few at home. However, that technology was getting obsolete as the touch-tone telephones came about. There was nothing necessarily wrong with the rotary telephones, except that they could not keep up with the new demands. And yes, rotary telephones were already an improvement from the times you had to call an operator so they would physically patch you to another number. Now imagine for a moment if somebody would have lobbied to keep the rotary phones and not let this other technology evolve?

From the touch tone then eventually we had more innovation that led to the early cordless phones, and cellular phones, and fast-forward all the way to today's smart phone. Yes, there was a "woke" person behind those innovations that was able to articulate that some of those technological advances needed to be modified and improved. Do you think they got push back from the established industries? They absolutely had A LOT of push back. Why do you think is that? Because it was going to disrupt their business model, that's why. These established industries had to either adapt, invest in changes to keep up or be left behind. Many of those now obsolete industries fought to keep the old systems, but ultimately, they failed. Now, if they would have used that time and energy (and money) to improve their own technology, then they would have not gone the way of the dodo. Keep this in mind as you read this book.

For all the innovations you see and enjoy today, there was a "woke" dude or gal who saw the potential for improvement and made it happen. If you're reading this in a tablet, in a computer, in a kindle, in a physical book, in a cell phone, in a web site, etc. It does not matter, the fact that my words are reaching you somehow there was somebody who had to fight an established industry to afford you the use of that innovation to improve your life. Yes, even reading. Back in the day there was quite a push to keep segments of the population analphabet.

Change is inevitable, and there are some who will prefer to keep you stagnated because it is self-serving to them, and their own industry or business model paradigm. And yes, that could even include some more theological aspects. This is nothing new, it has been going on for millennia. If there is a bias that can be exploited, somebody will come up with a way to manipulate their loyal followers into doing stuff that could very well be contrary to these loyal followers' best interests. It is actually tragically amusing to see it from the onset when you realize that. It is much like seeing an ant farm or any other corralled group of sentient beings being pushed through an artificially induced reality. However, this turns from amusing into callously devastating if people are starting to get hurt because of these bad policies.

In this book I will do my very best to try to open people's mind when it comes to this topic. After you finish reading this book you might very well continue to dislike the "woke" – but at least you will understand what are you are actually disagreeing with. Right now there is no consensus on what this "woke" is supposed to mean. And to be honest, I am not trying to imply that I will be the end-all-be all to give a definition to this paradigm. You will definitely have a lot more context for sure after reading this book though. What I will point out are the dangers that affect us all because of this misunderstanding. With that said, if you agree with my concept and definition, feel free to use it and share it based on my context and rationale. Better yet, please point them to my book (this or my other books). Whatever you do, please do not put words in my mouth. Anybody who does, I will just refer them to my book where I articulate things in the exact manner that I have deliberately expressed them.

Part of propaganda is to take things out of context, and therefore I will be caveating to ensure that my words are as accurate as possible. Therefore you will likely see some strategically placed redundancy in my statements. There is a reason for that. In that manner it is a lot harder for somebody to take my words out of context.

For you see, when things are real then it does not matter how complex something is. All the factors and all the circumstances are going to match perfectly no matter how you slice it, or what science you use. However, in a falsehood no matter how well-crafted it might be, the math will not add up somewhere. The concepts themselves will clash somewhere in the timeline when the truth is stretched. That is when you see people talking themselves into a corner. If they are truthful, they can speak your ear off for hours and days, the stories will not change the facts.

As we move forward through these pages, some of these concepts will feel contentious. Let me emphasize that I will not make any personal attacks. Even if you feel directly offended by my words. If you feel that way, just know that I am attacking an issue, a doctrine, or a concept <u>on the merits</u>.

We all have blind spots and might very well be victims of some of those concepts. If you do find yourself in that situation, do not worry. Often people feel offended if they are put on the spot, and it is *their own mind* what gets <u>them</u> upset. Facts are impervious to emotion. They are logical, measurable, and demonstrable. If you feel that way, try to look it from a third person's perspective and attribute the same metric to somebody you do not particularly like. It will help you be more objective as you read my words. However, you will ultimately need to return to face those demons with introspection. And yes, it might be a traumatic experience for some, because they will see themselves in a manner they have never realized before.

For this book I will not take any political stance either to the Left or Right side of the political spectrum. Though I know that these concepts, depending on where you live tend to have a high political charge to either side of the aforementioned political spectrum. In some places it will be very much to the right, and some will be very much to the left. There is north of 200 countries in the world (to include micronations), and they all have their own quirks and doctrines. This book is intended to be a bridge to link those extremes and find some common ground.

Surprisingly to some, I am not necessary for or against "woke" as a term – I am however against misinformation and manipulation. Some people, based on their own biased might call me "woke" – some might call me another epithet I rather do not describe as to not give any ideas to any haters out there. Some might appreciate what I have to say, because my intent is not to demonize any segment of the population. And yes, I will be speaking some truth onto some of those so called "too-woke" who tend to muddy the waters. The latter might be doing some mudding inadvertently, but it does happen. Therefore it is worth speaking about it in a pragmatic manner.

And pragmatism and the overhyped version of "*wokism*" are not synonymous. It is interesting to me, because I can, and have seen examples of people who overhype "woke" in a way that is so hyperbolic that it becomes a satirical version of itself. This of course will directly or indirectly have an effect on people that are contrary to whatever "good intentions" their "woke" narrative was trying to convey. And yes, I made the last sentence convoluted on purpose. I just wanted to illustrate how semantically speaking, ambiguity can be rampant if taken out of context. To clarify, this is what I meant. A person might have good intentions, but if they articulate those intentions in the erroneous manner, will be resulting in a counterproductive effect.

Can I make that less convoluted? Yes, I can. Sometimes people mean well, but end up saying something stupid. Even less convoluted? Sure, why not? What you say may carry unintended consequences. Can I make it more succinct? Sure. People misunderstand otherwise good intentions. I can go on, but now I am getting bored of the same example. Besides, I know my readers do not have problems with reading comprehension.

But unlike my readers, a lot of people out there do have problems processing information with a more dynamic degree of complexity. And that is when some people could become victims of believing a false narrative, just because it so happens to coincide with a particular world view, or under the scope of a narrow lens. We see this all the time. In politics, in the mainstream media, in independent media, by influencers, by the general public, by older and newer generations. In other words, everybody is vulnerable to these exploitable factors under the right conditions.

Decisions, however simple, are not binary. There are always several preliminary factors in play. Even if the final choice is binary, the factors leading to those choices were likely a lot more diverse. Most people will not be privy to understand those concepts. That is why propaganda works so well. And this concept of "woke" is very much instrumental for better or worse in the propagandistic narrative. That is both for and against propaganda. Which is a reason why it is important to shed some light onto this issue. This topic is a lot more important than what it seems to the general public. It is designed to seem menial, yet "threatening-lite." You will see what I mean by that as you read on the following chapters.

Just today I was reading some news from the United States that have politicians utilizing these terms as leverage for political gain. Unfortunate, yes. Unexpected, no. The United States much like any other country is composed of people, and people diverge in opinions. And in the gradient from each opinion people can get some half-truths implanted. These half-truths or in some instances outright lies will become key factors in their decision-making process. It is a very simple concept, but it is very complex in execution. That is why it is so easy to conceal misdirection if people do not know what to look for. In other words, it is hard to ask a question if you did not know that there was an inquire to make in the first place.

I for one always have had a skeptical mind. Despite this, at some points in my life I too have been both naïve and overconfident on things that I was not fully cognizant about. And that it is fine and expected. We all have blind spots, and sometimes you need to fall flat in order to recognize any shortcomings. In fact, I would argue that if you don't ever get challenged there is a healthy chance that you have been delusional or you could be victim of your own grandiosity.

For example, did you know that it is easier to manipulate a person who thinks they know everything there is to know about something? Why do you think is that? Simple answer, because they already psyched themselves as all-knowing. This makes it a lot easier for another person [who likely does not have their best interest in mind] to convince this know-it-all that they are spot on in their [erroneous] assumptions. Do that long enough and it will erode their critical thinking and intellectual honesty from the inside out. In other words, they will get convinced of a false reality. To make it even clearer, they will fall into what is known as the echo chamber.

And I realize some of these topics might sound a lot more convoluted than what we normally assess to be related to "woke" in the common colloquial terms. That is exactly why this has sparked my attention and I've decided to look into it. Here in this book I present to you my findings on this research. Again, I do not intent for you to take my words as the end-all-be all, but I do expect to spark your interest to start a dialog that is deeper than the shallow talking points being tossed around.

As with most of my writing, this is best read with an open mind. If you are familiar with my style of writing I will pull your mind in all directions and come full circle from all sides. Much like spokes in a bicycle wheel. The intent is not to disorient you, but to ensure you can see the context from all different directions.

Whomever wants to manipulate you is very happy if you see the world in a very one-dimensional manner. That is the reason why propaganda works, and the way it is designed. Although we will discuss about propaganda in this book, I am more interested in elaborating how this particular topic is used as a catalyst to empower a propagandist... The charlatan, if you will. The good news is that by understanding this context in a holistic manner, the propagandist (charlatan) will have a much harder time in their attempt to bamboozle you.

And learning to identify the truth in a sea of falsehoods it is the main reason why this book came to life. Enjoy the ride!

CHAPTER 1

IS 'WOKE" A BAD THING? |
You Might Be Surprised

Short answer, it depends on what you are understanding by the "woke" terminology. If you are against "woke" because it is indeed questioning your motives and able to show that you are in the wrong, then very likely "woke" will not be a welcoming world view. In contrast, if you are the one who is advocating for a change because you or those you care about have been disenfranchised, then "woke" will be a very welcoming thing in your life. The catch is that the term has been so misappropriated that it will make it very hard to define in a holistic context. Miring this situation is of course convenient for those who want to get away with certain wicked things. For example, if they do not want a group of people to realize that a narrative or action is against their best interests. In other words, those who demonize "woke" have something to hide or prefer to keep it unclear from the public view. Others might go to the opposite extreme and use "woke" as a social justice term which defends situations that do not warrant a defense in the first place. Neither of these extremes is helpful, because it detracts from what is indeed intended by "woke." What a conundrum! Where to start? How about some actual definitions and history? From here everything else follows. This chapter is exactly about that.

In this chapter we will use actual dictionary definitions and historical colloquialisms in regards to "woke." You would think that has been done already in mainstream media and politics, right? Well, not quite, it has not been consistent. And there is a reason, because it has a potential to create visceral responses on people, therefore it becomes the perfect catalysts to move rhetoric into action if it is misunderstood, and the actual definition becomes elusive.

Once we define the terms in this chapter, this is the definition and premise that we will utilize for the rest of the chapters in this book. You will see why. It will help us provide context on why this can be such a controversial situation, when in reality it has been hijacked as a target of opportunity.

Dictionary Definition:

WOKE. *Verb. Past of Wake*

WAKE. *Verb. 3rd person present - **Wakes**; past tense **Waked**; gerund or present participle **Waking**; past participle **Woken**.*

1. *Emerge of cause to emerge from a state of sleep; stop sleeping*
2. *Become alert or aware of*
3. *Cause (something) to stir or come to life*

Synonyms:

WOKE. Awakened, stirred, roused, wakened, aroused

Thesaurus

WOKE. Awakened (v.), awakened, stirred, roused, weakened, aroused, wake up (Dictionary Form), Come around (Dictionary Form), Get up (Dictionary Form), Come to (Dictionary Form), Aroused (v.), Aroused, stirred, awakened, roused, kindled, challenged, awoke (v.) awoke, aroused, awakened wakened, wake up (Dictionary Form), Come Alive (Dictionary Form).

Antonym

Stifled. Quiet, muffled, muted, soft, silent.

Colloquial definition:

WOKE. Another way to characterize someone woke is as "hip" or "open-minded."

Other Usages:

WOKE. In activism and politics used in the context of "alert to racial prejudice and discrimination."

"Woke" gained resurgence occurred in the 2010s as a result of many social inequalities that were existent but normalized through the span of many years. But circa and before that, the term "woke" was also being used as a slang to satirize and uncover other pop-culture situations such as "catfishing," or exaggerating wealth, pretentiousness, petulance, pedantry, cheating on a "significant other," or any other *non-quite-malign* deceptive tactics. In other words, calling people out if they were trying to portray themselves as somebody they are not. In fact, there was no shortage of memes and even comedy routines that were intended to uncover those particular instances of unauthenticity.

However, as many inequalities continued to brew for many years. This caused our societies to become more and more polarized. This phenomenon did not occur by chance. In fact, there was a lot of politics and [unsurprising to some] religious doctrines that contributed for and against this archetype. And sadly, that is by design. Politics and religion are very strong catalysts and can get people to rally for or against a doctrine. They create a visceral response to many people, and more importantly, it gives the perception of justified actions, even if the actions are not wholesome. And we have observed these tactics in action, where some actions seem to justify the means in the minds of certain followers. Of course, those actions do have consequences and people found guilty of committing crimes have been prosecuted. Yes, even though the people who committed these crimes were under the impression that they were serving a higher authority. And this is another reason why this is so dangerous.

Most people see the world through a very narrow lens. This narrow lens represents their own perception of reality. Much like seeing something through a key-hole or the viewfinder of a static camera.

There might be something that seems to either support or deny a claim based on that small context. However, when a doctrine is based on falsehoods the math is not going to add up somewhere. No matter how well-crafted this falsehood intends to be. Conversely, when something its true, it does not matter how you try to conceal it, there is always another way to validate a truthful claim. Though the latter might take a very long time. Even years or centuries later. And we know this to be true, because we have been able to compare ancient records with older beliefs, and we can categorically demonstrate their gaps of knowledge.

And the truth is that doing so is not all that complicated. Especially nowadays with the copious amounts of information and recording devices in virtually everybody's hands. That means that we have a lot of witnessing points-of-view to demonstrate empirically the truthfulness or a falsehood of an event. That does not mean that you won't find somebody who will gaslight people into not believing empirical evidence. There is a reason for that, of course. It is inconvenient for those who are pushing a narrative that is contrary to the evidence.

From there is when things can start getting very dark. And we'll talk about that shortly. Keep this in mind as we continue with the context. Hopefully, by now you have been able to realize how things can be misconstrued under this term. If it is not obvious enough, it became a political football. And to me, that is actually very disgusting. Why? Because innocent people get involved in the middle of all these neo-cultural wars.

So, to recap. The term *woke* means in essence that the "woke" person is paying attention. In other words he or she is not asleep. If you are asleep, by definition you are not paying attention; we are more vulnerable when we are snoozing. Then the term moved as part of the vernacular to poke fun to those pretentious people who were not authentic. But as the geopolitical situation around the world became more polarized, it morphed into a tool for social justice by virtue of shedding some light onto situations that were unsavory, however *normalized*. And that last word "normalized" is key.

Of course for those who were not disenfranchised, this sense of normality was ok. In their world-views vantage point it did not need to change at all. Why should it? It was working fine for *them*. But the world is a lot more complex than that. And while there are some who are living in relative peace and/or luxury, there is also a societal segment who lives in the opposite reality. Let these realities span for long enough and nobody will think anything of it, because *it is what it is*. That does not mean that it is acceptable for those who have been dealt the bad hand. The interesting fact is that some of those who were dealt a bad hand might have not even known any better. This "ignorance is bliss" can turn on a dime if suddenly there is an understanding of *unjustified* inequality. And another key word is "unjustified." As you will notice, the context wheel keeps getting more and more complex. That is why it is easy to bamboozle people who do not understand this complexity.

And that brings another problem. Some people refuse to understand actual facts, even if it is against their own best interests. And now that we have explained this, let us move on to the gloomier part on the "woke" evolution.

The term "woke" was colloquially used as an adjective. In other words a description term in African-American Vernacular English (AAVE). For example: "This young boy is '*woke*' *[woken]* and won't buy the same bullshit his parents did when they were his age."

Based on the context the same word "woke" can also be used as a noun. In other words a subject. For example: "This emerging '*woke*' has a generational understanding of issues inconvenient to those who seek to disenfranchise them."

Subsequently, woke continue to evolve and encompassed other disenfranchised segments of society. All these are segments that were otherwise condoned or even expected to be used as either a joke's punchline or were often deemed as second-class citizens. A few examples include but are not limited to: Sexism, racism, homophobia, antisemitism, segregation, social inequality, birth origin, disability, etc.

And to be against any of these groups mentioned, you would have to admit it would make a person a pretty dubious individual. However, there are political and religious doctrines that indeed advocate for giving stark differences in the way people in any of those segments should be treated. Of course placing a privileged class of individuals on top and the disenfranchised on the bottom. And if the individuals on the bottom complain, then those on top will quash even their very argument for daring complaining. Even if the complaint is civil and peaceful. And that is how situations can bring more friction between these segments. This is nothing new, it has been going on for millennia.

This is not a black-against-white people issue at its core. That is incidental, and it is a lot more complex than that. Of course, those who want to manipulate will paint in such a simplistic way. It is convenient, it is easy to remember, and it helps those with a narrow vision scope to fly off the handle without really understanding the intricacies; or even the fact that the more short-sighted segment of this dichotomy have become useful fools.

For the United States of America, yes, there is a "Black versus White" people dichotomy in the heart of "woke" at this point in time. But that is incidental based on the history of our country. We cannot condemn the current generation for the mistakes our ancestors did. That is unfair and unproductive. It then becomes a cause for friction. Besides, in countries where there is less diversity than the United States, the disenfranchised people have the same color skin as their oppressors. I know this can be hard to understand for some, but it is because they will see it from their own vantage point. But the truth is that inequality is a lot more complex, and has been going on for millennia.

Let me give you two semi-contemporary examples so you can understand what I mean by this. In the Soviet Union, it was the party who was oppressive to the rest of the proletarian. The Soviet people all had the same skin color in the same geographical areas they lived, but there was a very wide distinction of who was on top or who was in the bottom of the hierarchy – despite their "equality." Another example, in China when Mao Zedong was in power and following the rubric from the Soviet Union, same thing. They were all Chinese citizens, yet they were all divided in very distinct social classes (even within certain ethnicities). Those at the top of the party were a lot better off than those at the bottom. Of course that under that system they pretended to act as though everybody was treated as equal. That was not the case.

In my book about authoritarianism and propaganda you can read a lot more examples. And the reason why I bring this up it is because that particular division between ethnicities in the United States of America is what makes this division all the more incendiary. And the fact is that the world is polarized, and it has been polarizing more and more in the last few years. And America is no exception. Polarization to an extend it is inevitable. Not everybody is going to agree on everything, does not matter what it is. And the problem is that there are opportunists who will be able to rally people's visceral responses to follow a skewed reality. Let us explore more to see how that works.

As the United States was getting more and more polarized in the 2010's the injustices that happened against minorities and other groups continued to occur. The difference is that today we have a lot more recording devices and there is a way to put information out to the world in a matter of seconds, or even broadcast it live.

In other words technology. People in positions of power have been abusing their authority from the beginning of human civilization. The problem is that there was seldom a chance to give a witness account, let alone a photographic or videographic witness account. For example if they were torturing somebody, that person being tortured would not live to tell the story. Or if something as done behind legal proceeding, the context, and the full scope of investigation, even with empirical evidence was going to end up murkier if there were some skillful attorney loopholes.

What do I mean by that? Let us say that there was a case of police brutality. And the police officer was in fact guilty, but during the legal proceedings the prosecutor made a mistake, or was not as good, or as prepared the defense attorney; then this case of police brutality would go into legal impunity based on a technicality. A technicality is not the same as an empirical reality. People have been found guilty and sent to capital punishment under a court of law, just to realize years after they committed a state-sponsored-killing to a prisoner who was in fact innocent.

It can go both ways. There could be a criminal who is caught red handed. But due to some technicalities or other fallacies during the trial, then the criminal gets to walk the streets free to try again. And yes, this happens quite often.

So, understanding this, this inequality under the law is what gave a segway to the Black Lives Matter (BLM) movement. And for the United States of America, this became an increasingly divisive catalyst when in reality was a call for awareness. But you know, semantics. And keeping black people quiet has been unfortunately historically convenient to a significant segment of the population.

There is a reason why I put a warning before you open my books. I am going to speak some facts, and some of these facts might rock your world. But you will be better in the other end, I promise. *If* you are intellectually honest.

There are propagandists who want to demonize black people or any other minority. In other words, racism does exist. Not only in America, but around the world. In America we have a lot of empirical history to demonstrate that black people have been disenfranchised. They are not the only ones, but we cannot ignore the fact that for many generations black people were denied the same rights as any other American Citizen. And yes, there are racist people in power, in main-stream media, or any other platform of influence. The latter could be working behind the scenes. The goal is simple, but complex in execution. Keep people who were in the lower echelons quiet and calm. And for those disenfranchised to keep accepting the fact they were second class citizens. Give them an illusion of being equal, but rig the system against them.

It is clear as day for those who understand it. But the situation of disenfranchising has been normalized for so long that it also became part of the very fabric of society. And these groups of disenfranchised people were simply asking for their human rights to be respected. Be equal under the law and afforded the same opportunities as everyone else to become the person they are meant to be based on their own merits.

This narrative of course got skewed in propaganda. There was no shortage of talking heads starting to implant misinformation onto other people. Some of this misinformation was very well crafted, and for unsuspecting good people, it would make perfect sense. Of course, they are only factoring reality with a very narrow scope of data points. If the audience would understand the entire context, these propagandists very well know that their narrative is unsupportable (hopefully, there are some bad people out there too).

In fact, that is why a lot of people who are very much onboard with diversity would feel mistreated and offended as though they were been designated as racists. Most of these, otherwise very nice people were fed misinformation, and were factoring their understanding based on very much cherrypicked talking points. It was designed that way. Why? Well, two words. Power and money.

There is a lot of money on disharmony. Let me give you an example. Let us say there is a movie plot. And in this movie, everybody is getting along, everybody agrees, and everybody is singing kumbaya, end of movie. Who in their right mind wants to watch that? Unless it is a promotional film for some weird utopian cult. Conversely, when a movie has some sort of conflict it gets a more appealing storyline. It can be a jealousy driven plot, maybe an action flick of a hero going against all odds, it could be a story of survival, something. In other words, a character arc, even if the antagonist is portrayed as weak. Whatever the case, it needs to have a hook and a plot to move the story along. Same with propaganda. There is going to be an antagonist. The difference is that the audience could at some point be asked to rally and defend against this antagonist. And yes, that does happen.

Understanding this, you can see how the waters can easily murk if somebody wants to control a narrative with misinformation. The first step will be character assassination. Especially if the "woke" person is onto something that would be inconvenient if it was deciphered by the general public. Much like an illusionist, they will show you the "magic trick" from one side, but they will not show you "how they perform" the trick from *their* vantage point. Similar principle but a lot more elaborated.

In the next chapter I will speak about the "woke" timeline. That way you can see how these events are not occurring in a vacuum. There is a reason for everything that we see going on. Sadly, some people will become useful fools. And spoiler alert, we are all vulnerable to fall under this trap. But the more we understand context and open our minds, the more we will be able to raise above the noise and realize the reality. Buckle up, because it is about to get more mind-blowing in the next chapters.

CHAPTER 2

HISTORICAL REFERENCES |
"Woke" Defined

In the previous chapter I gave you the dictionary and colloquial definitions for "woke." But this word is more complex than that. In this chapter we will define it for what it does to society. The intent is to give this term a common ground that is logical, measurable, and demonstrable. Further, we will explore the timeline of how this word has evolved and the geopolitical causations and co-relations with the use of this term. That way we can mitigate confusions as we set the premise for this argument. There is no debate. It is what it is. We can demonstrate these as historical facts. You are welcome to agree or disagree with the motives and execution of these events, but they occurred and we cannot change that. With that said, we can always learn from the mistakes others have made. This does not mean that we are responsible for mistakes made by our ancestors. But we are very much responsible for the mistakes we make today.

When you stop and see this situation for what it is, the ramifications are mind-bending. For the casual observer and consumer of news the historical correlations and links will seem as though they are disconnected. I've said it before and I will say it again. It is designed to be that way.

In the previous chapter we cover a lot of information. But mind you, this was only scratching the surface in order to ease you in into the many intricacies. The reality is that understanding the full scope will be akin to drinking from a firehose. Again, it is designed to be that way. Whomever wants to control the narrative will pepper you with so many talking points and conjectures that people will either go numb, or are bound to get confused. That is why I designed the book in the way I did. I'll introduce you to some topics, and then we will explore each in a way that is more palatable. The benefit to you is that it will open your mind to what is otherwise hidden from view. My intent is to incentivize your critical thinking and intellectual honesty. And no, you do not have to agree with *me*. You have to agree or disagree with the *facts*.

For us to embark in this journey, let us understand that other antonyms (opposite meaning) for "woke" include: slumbered, snoozed, retired, turned-in, conked off, or conked out.

In other words, you are either awake or you are not awake. Which choice would you rather take? Keep in mind that blissful ignorance is tacit consent for somebody who is in fact awake to make unmitigated decisions on your behalf while you snooze. So I ask you again, which choice would you rather take?

Realize that even those who dissent might be the "woke" ones against their opposition. Again, this can become a semantic game to some, but in reality, it ends up being two opposing points of view advocating for their perceived reality. Which one is correct? That can be a loaded question. Because sometimes it can be either one of them – if they hold the facts – or at any degree of correctness or erroneousness. In some cases it could be neither of them, and both sides are fighting windmills (Don Quixote reference), or it could be both of them agreeing, yet fighting against each other. That later one happens more often than you think.

That is why in most authoritarian regimes from the past, when the people finally "woke up" – the authoritarian fell. Because an authoritarian is only as strong as his or her followers. That is why they will cherry pick the information that their followers will be afforded to use in order to factor "their decisions." It is not the followers' decisions; the decisions were already made for them. That is yet another reason why some followers could in effect become useful fools.

Let us explore how "woke" has evolved through time.

Timeline in American Culture:

1860: The first recorded, though lesser-known use of this terminology in political activism was circa Abraham Lincoln's presidential election. Lincoln was in fact a Republican candidate. Around the time "woke" was used as "awake" in a paramilitary youth organization known as the "Wide Awakes" in Connecticut. This group grew rapidly through northern states as it was advocating for abolition of slavery. This was not convenient to the Southern states at the time, because slavery was not only condoned, but very much integral to their economic model. The Southern states were also not happy about the fact that this group was also largely composed of Black Americans.

In the event you were not aware, the abolition of slavery was the main reason why the American Civil War started and was fought from April 12, 1861 to May 26, 1865. Northerner states (also known as the Union) largely were against slavery as a form of economic income, either directly or derivative from slave labor. Southern states, unfortunately, were perfectly ok with slave labor as part of their economic model at that time. That is why the Confederacy was created and subsequently the Civil War started. Though the Civil War in the South was known (and for some still known) as the "War of Northern Aggression." Now you know.

And that's when the gaslighting starts. Some will say it was about economy and states' rights. Which begs the question, economy based on what? And states' rights to do what? The answer to both questions is human beings as private property. That is why so many people take exception when Southerner people fly the Confederate *Battle* flag. This symbol of *heritage* Southerner people claim, unfortunately for many around the world also represent the fact that lives were lost and slavery was condoned under that banner (and other similar or lesser-known banners). Also, because succession from the United States of

America is technically high-treason under the law… if you see things very pragmatically.

But the end of the Civil War was not the end of black people disenfranchisement. They were not slaves to a plantation, but now they were slaves to a system of discrimination. And yes, there was rampant racism and prosecution of minorities by those who were very much enamored with the premise of defending the Confederacy views on slavery. Please do not feel offended if speaking about the Confederacy touches a nerve. You are not responsible for what your ancestors did. But we are all very much responsible for what we do today.

1923: Jamaican philosopher and social activist Marcs Garvey wrote "Wake up Ethiopia! Wake up Africa!" Garvey also uses this concept to spread other ideas using this situation as a metaphor. This was very much during the Jim Crow era. And if you know anything about that (we'll talk more about it). American Black people were very much discriminated against. Racism was rampant, and in essence legal and condoned. Black people suffered lynchings and other horrible injustices under a system that did not at all have their best interest in mind.

Jim Crow laws were in effect from the late 19th Century until the 1960's. The first known use of the phrase "Jim Crow" was in 1884 in a newspaper describing a congressional debate. Notice that the Civil War ended in 1865. The term "Jim Crow" is attributed to a white actor who performed in black face named Thomas D. Rice, and performed a song-dance derogatory depiction of black people called "Jump Jim Crow." Yeah, I know the more you learn, the more disgusting the way the old days used to be. We take a lot of our diversity for granted today. That was not the case just a few decades ago. And although today we do have some vestigial remains of those unsavory days, we are all the future of the country. Hence, it is incumbent on us all to make it better for us all - together.

1938: Lead Belly (real name Huddie Ledbetter) was a Black American folk singer-songwriter used the words "stay woke" on his song "Scottsboro Boys." The song speaks about the real story of two young black men who were wrongfully accused of raping two white women in Alabama. The song serves as a warning of potential racially motivated dangers of white America to black people. If you are familiar with the history of segregation, it was definitely not safe for black people. Racially motivated crimes against blacks were all too common and dehumanizing. There was unfortunately a very wide erroneous consensus that white people were superior to blacks. And it is worth mentioning that no race is superior, period. We are all human beings.

Despite this, entire families were terrorized and that included massacres due to lynching or other reprehensive crimes against humanity. Living under this fear, it was logical that most people would choose safety over speaking truth to power.

Political power was rigged against black Americans. The act of sharing the same space even in a bus or public establishment was legally forbidden. Let alone the right to vote; it was out of the question as black people were consider second-class citizens. Literature, and even early cartoons from that era condone discrimination and ridiculed most minorities with scatting racial depictions.

But I will say it again. You cannot be held responsible for the terrible things the previous generations did. But you are very much responsible for your actions today.

1962: The Oxford English Dictionary adds the word "woke" with the meaning: Well-informed or aware, especially in a political of cultural sense.

The dictionaries cites the early usage to an article titled "If you're woke You Dig It." The author was African-American novelist William Melvin Kelley.

1964 & 1965: Congress passed the Civil Rights Act of 1964 and Voting Rights Act of 1965. This finally occurred after and despite the fact several Southerner lawmakers were filibustering the process. Fortunately it passed with bipartisan support. And yes, this is despite the fact that the Supreme Court ruled unanimously in 1954, ten years earlier, that public school segregation was unconstitutional.

This comes to show that <u>most</u> Americans are indeed good decent people who treat everybody with respect and want to improve the lives of <u>all</u> citizens. However, there is a group of people who will stonewall the effort and put sand in the gears of progress. Meanwhile, while these political games were being played, we also had two World Wars, which by the way also had African-Americans serving in uniform for a system that considered them second-class citizens. All they wanted was what Dr. Martin Luther King advocated for. To be treated as equal human beings, and be judged by their merits and not by the color of their skin.

Unsurprisingly, Dr. King was assassinated by somebody who was a racist, and would not accept that we are all human beings.

1967: Barry Beckman used the line "I been sleeping all my life. And now that Mr. Garvey done woke me up, I'm gon' stay woke. And I'm gon help him wake up other black folk." This was part of the play "Garvey Lives!" which had political connotations.

And spoiler alert, not because the civil acts right was passed it means that African Americans and other minorities did not remain disenfranchised. The arsenal to weaponize racial division is a lot more sinisterly creative than most people realize. There are ways to make the legal system work in favor of an oppressive system. For example: Economically, by introducing vices or other detractions, lack of resources, compromise the level of education, foment a social divide (that does exist). And even though we are a lot better than most countries, remember what I said. It is not everybody in the country who are doing something despicable. It only takes a <u>small group</u> of people to do so in order to slow down the entire system. That is why I am writing an entire book (this book) about it, so we do not fall for that trap.

2016: Singer Childish Gambino uses "woke" as a reference to infidelity in his song "Redbone." This term, although dormant for several decades also included alertness to social and/or racial injustice and/or discrimination.

2008: The song "Master Teacher" sung by soul singer Erykah Badu says "I stay woke." The song makes a reference to self-awareness, inquisitiveness and being motivated for something better. Even though the song is not directly singing about social justice. However, the Merriam-Webster dictionary credits her for connections to social issues. And I can understand the correlation, because sometimes a meaning even in metaphor can yield the same correlation to a greater denotation.

But I would be remiss if I did not mention that the song "Master Teacher" was actually composed by songwriter Georgia Anne Muldrow in 2005. She attributed the theme to staying up, literally not passing out. Maybe she did not intent do use "woke" in the sense the Merriam-Webster dictionary took, but it was certainly inspiring.

2012: The Russian feminist rock group Pussy Riot was imprisoned for protesting against the Putin regime. The hashtag #Staywoke and #FreePussyRiot started to trend. Erykah Badu wrote in her social media *"Truth requires no belief. Stay Woke. Watch closely. #FreePussyRiot.*

2014: Black Lives Matter (BLM) used the term *"stay woke"* in the aftermath of the shooting of Michael Brown in 2014.

2015: The term "woke" became an internet meme, and its trend was growing in Google searches. And unfortunately, that is when it started to get the waters muddied by contemporary opportunistic entities. Some who were very much in favor of having "woke" as a social justice catalyst for the benefit of society, and others who would character assassinate "woke" to make it a parody of itself. And of course there were many in the middle not really understanding the connotation and making it worse for either extreme. It has been eight years since then by the time I'm writing this manuscript. How many young people in their early 20's you think they will remember these intricacies? If they are 20 now, that means they were twelve years old. Think about it.

2016: Black Entertainment Television (BET) cable TV channel airs the documentary Stay Woke. In there they speak about the BLM movement and how the colloquialism grew politically and socially aware by activists.

As the term continued to gain popularity with left-leaning groups it was no coincidence that it became a polarizing factor in the political discourse. By this time American President Trump was elected and it is no secret that many around the world considered him a very polarizing figure. Love or hate the guy, that is not the issue here. The fact is that his time in office was an important factor in the way some narratives that were otherwise dormant came to the forefront like a tsunami. Sure, if you were a consumer of right-leaning news you might have not seen it the same way, but if you were consuming not just left-leaning news, but world-news who are not aligned with U.S. politics, you would be surprised (perhaps) how differently right-leaning perception of reality was in contrast with the rest of the planet.

This time of course created an opportunity for propagandists to deceivingly equate those asking for "fairness" as an "attack to America." Very different dynamics, however, there was visceral response and the words from propagandists were very well-crafted to elicit those visceral responses. I'll speak more about those techniques in a future chapter. But for now, understand that if a pretty talking head is saying something on your media of choice, they were likely given a script to hit certain key phrases in order to glue your eyeballs to the screen.

The propagandist would amplify any misconstructions to the main message, especially if they could get a sound-bite from somebody saying something stupid. And yes, people with good intentions could say or do something stupid. And now, *this* sound bite has become an exhibit for the propagandists' efforts.

However, the American political climate on the left was also to blame for the fact that more centrist democrats would actually try to distance themselves from the newer generations of Democratic leaders. Sure that some new left-leaning leaders needed more mentorship and guidance. That is something that did not happen optimally, and hence some right-wing heavy hitters were able to run rampant with propaganda that polarized the democratic party more and more. Especially because the democratic party was not listening to the new generation. And spoiler alert, the new generation is who will ultimately inherit the country; therefore they have a vested interest in their future. And yes, that is treacherous to those who want to keep things the way they are. The last generation was pretty much asleep at the wheel, and that was very convenient for charlatans.

2017: Columnist David Brooks wrote "to be woke is to be radically aware and justifiably paranoid. It is to be cognizant of the rot pervading the power structure."

Sociologist Marcyliena Morgan wrote "while coolness is empty of meaning and interpretation and displays no particular consciousness, woke is explicit and direct regarding injustice, racisms, sexism, etc."

2018: African-American journalist Sam Sanders asserted that "woke" was lost due to overuse by white liberals and a co-option by business in an attempt to appear progressive. This is being known as woke-washing, and of course it stands against what "woke" was supposed to be. I can see what he means by that, because I was definitely paying attention to the socio-political climate back in 2018, but I do not fully agree with his point of view, though I think it does have so merits.

In other words, the way I assess it is that "woke" became a meme of itself, because propagandists were able to exploit the willfully ignorant and create enough distraction to muddy the waters. Surely some of the well-intentioned people who saw this as an opportunity to either get some clout, and others to become parasitical as the trend evolved were also catalysts in satirizing "woke." Which is actually a very heartbreaking situation, because it robs the merit it was supposed to have several decades back during the times of emancipation.

2019: By this time "woke" has been used as a satire of itself on all kinds of platforms. And it is a trend that continues to this day. This was a tactic used by those opposed to progressive social movements. Some would use disparaging descriptions such as "over righteous liberalism." This scornful trope equates "woke" with what British journalist Steven Poole mentioned as "following and intolerant and moralistic ideology."

In American Politics it is used mostly by the right-wing as an insult against left-wing people, and even from political-centrist against certain segments of their own demographics and the Democratic party. In the following chapters I will talk more about how these have been morphed and been received around the current geopolitical spectrum. Both in the United States and around the world. It is very likely that if somebody from the right-wing sees the word "woke" it will equate with some off-the-handle liberal world-view, when in fact right-leaning people can also be considered "woke" in their own doctrines. And yes, we will talk about how those situations very much happen. The weaponization of this word has been very much abused, and as its meaning keeps getting muddied out, it is important to remember what it was supposed to be in the first place, and what are the factors which contributed to character assassinate an otherwise legitimate concern.

Present Day: (at the time this manuscript was written):

The demonization of the term "woke" of course continues to this day. By the time I am writing this book it is March 2023 (and ended in May 2023).   I do not presume this will be done overnight, much less that it would not be further weaponized and exploited by both left and right leaning people to galvanize their agendas. And the fact is that as with any type of leaning there is a trending appeal, but these appeals could very well have very low shelf-lives and disappear as a passing fashion style and become nothing but a footnote in the fabric of society.

There was plenty of opportunism that saw the appeal "woke" has – especially to millennials. Merchandise, plot points inserted in movie scripts, influencers, and even their archnemesis, etc. They all rode the *Woke wagon* as part of their marketing technique.   Today's currency is attention, and this was something the opportunists could identify with and gain their target audience's attention. But as with anything else in life, once a situation gets too big to control, then some dialing-down will occur to keep it contained.   Especially if this starts to become inconvenient for other more established parties.

One of those desperate attempts to curtail it was a campaign that was asserting the slogan "get woke, go broke." Think about it for a second. What does that tell you? Is that true or is not true? I'll give you a few moments, meet me in the paragraph below.

In case you didn't realize it, it is pure propaganda.   It is advertisement posted by other competing industries whereas "woke" is not convenient, because that means people will figure out a better option.   Cleverly written, and it even rhymes. Propaganda can be unsavory, but that does not mean it is not catchy. That's why it resonates so well with their specific target audiences.

The term "Woke Capitalism" coined by writer Ross Douthat saying something along the lines that "brands used politically progressive messaging as substitute for genuine reform." And there is some truth to that. Especially if the brand is just using this to exploit the target audience's bias as a metric of appeal towards their brand. And yes, this happens, not just to "woke" but pretty much with everything that is available with or without a price tag. Remember the actual currency is attention.

Cultural scientists Akane Kani and Rosalind Gill mentioned something along the lines that if "woke" in advertisement gets out of control, then the very things they claim to protect will receive backlash. They go on to say that race, gender, religion, etc. then become mascots in advertisement, and they will actually suffer negative consequence despite some of the Neoliberal attempts to protect them.

By now you probably realized the obvious. There is a lot to gain by whomever gets to control the narrative. "Woke" started as a sense of awareness against being disenfranchised. Then it became a trope to insult people with a different political leaning. At least in the United States of America. Many other countries have demonized "woke" a long time ago, even if it was not called the same thing. But rather it was given the same treatment to any term if there was any thought that someone was speaking out of turn; then that would have been considered "woke," and therefore not allowed in a repressive society.

Can this "woke" thing get out of control by people who overuse it in any context? Absolutely, and you can say the same for anything you have. Can you overuse a computer? Sure, you can use to do some actual work, or waste all day surfing for stuff that is designed to waste time. Can you overuse a car? Sure, you can drive from A to B as needed, or you can be that asshole who puts everybody out on the road in danger by driving too close or speeding with total disregard for others. Can you overuse your phone? Sure, you can use it to access your apps and keep in touch with all the people and entities you need to function in today's society, or you can be socially inept and stay with your nose buried in your phone when you are in the company of other living-breathing human beings in a social setting.

For the more conservative people. Can you overuse a gun? Sure, you can use it for self-defense and peace of mind, or there are most definitely those dangerous trigger-happy-morons who go on mass shooting rampages. It happens every other day. There are mass shootings in the United States of America constantly. Even in the very ship I am floating as I type this, we conduct drills in the event of mass shooters. Is that worse than being woke? How? The point is that <u>anything</u> that has a designed purpose can be misused by parasitical opportunists.

Now that you know the origins and how this has been exploited, let us turn our attention to understand who gets to benefit from woke being mischaracterized. And yes, there are plenty of people who get to benefit from this. And it is not too farfetched that some of those opposed would ride this trend in order to skew it. We know this happens, because we have seen it throughout history. And yes, some people will want to prevent you from learning history for the very same reason. Though they will use some straw-man argument to justify their need "to protect the children" from whatever imaginary foe they find convenient.

Yes, we will talk about that soon. And spoiler alert, it might make you feel offended. But if you're not "woke" then you should be ok, right? But if you are indeed "woke," then this might or might not come to you as a surprise. But still you might learn something. See you in Chapter 3.

CHAPTER 3

THE INCONVENIENT TRUTH|
Who Benefits when Demonizing the "Woke?"

"In cases of authoritarianism the authoritarian needs a foe in order to cling to power." – J. Marcelo Baqueroalvarez, 2023.
"Woke" in its true form is the actual adversary the authoritarian fears the most. Why? Because it means the cherry picked "truth" points spewed in their rhetoric were <u>not</u> the only actual points available to the public in general with full context. In other words, the authoritarian gives a very redacted version of their intentions to their followers. The "woke" could very well provide additional data points that the followers were not privy under the propaganda authorized by the authoritarian. It is not convenient for the authoritarian. The authoritarian followers trail a distorted reality painted as truth. Only very few at the very top of some echelons know the intricacies of the scheme. That same courtesy is not provided to those in the bottom who will ultimately have to do the dirty work. Yes, I am being redundant on purpose because this point is what keeps getting missed over and over again. How do you combat "woke" if you are an authoritarian? Deny the very existence of any down checks to your doctrine, and if you cannot do that, then you demonize any criticism, so your followers will discard any dissention outright, or at least learn about it with a prominently implanted bias in your favor. To that end, propagandists will have all the pretty talking heads on their corners spewing very specific buzz words and talking points. Welcome to the reality of the world that you been living all along.

The first question you should ask if somebody is calling somebody "woke" in a derogatory way should be, why are

you so afraid about what this "woke" person has to say? Seems pretty obvious to me. Pragmatically speaking, if the woke person is indeed an idiot, then whatever platitudes they say will not convince the followers because there will be no merit to those claims. However, if there is indeed merit to those claims, the propagandist will immediately and quite intensively start a character assassination campaign against the person they find threatening to their authority and influence.

People are impressionable, and those with an exploitable bias tend to be even more vulnerable to follow tropes implanted by the pretty talking heads in their preferred method of consuming media. It does not matter in what form it comes, the talking points will be very similar even in their uniqueness, because they serve the same purpose. That purpose is to confuse the followers and implant a false reality that will galvanize their obedience and unparallel support.

Are some of those followers' terrible people? Statistically, yes, that is a possibility. There are good and bad people everywhere in the world. But consider that <u>someone</u> trying to have a better world for <u>everyone</u> is not by definition a bad person.

With that said, a person might have good intentions but fall short in the execution of a plan, or the very articulation of those intentions. And that is possible, good intentions alone mean nothing if the plan is not viable. Also, even a well-intentioned deed if it turns authoritarian then it has already negated its benevolence by the fact that it is authoritarian in nature and principle. A very fancy way to say that every extreme is dangerous. Unlimited power fosters corruption, and this tends to be accompanied closely or distantly by a high degree of delusion. In other words, people who climb too high onto unlimited power lose sense of reality because they are seeing the world from their own very limited bubble. And in this bubble, you can be certain that anyone allowed is required to be a "yes man or woman."

And you will see this "yes man or woman" play a very pivotal role in the enforcing of any nefarious agenda. Authoritarians tend to be shrewd on the onset, but it is not sustainable long term. The reason is because the higher they move onto the food chain, the fewer check and balances they get. In *their mind*, they think they are the smartest person in the room. However, we have seen through history that the longer an authoritarian has been in power unchallenged, the more paranoid and erratic they tend to become. Especially if this cavalier period of abuses has been sustained long enough. That means there is a huge chance that illegal or otherwise criminal deeds have happened under their watch, or directly mandated by this authoritarian.

Then one day, the authoritarian will wake up and realize the obvious. They have done enough shady stuff that if they lose power, there will be a lot of enemies seeking revenge. Every single event of authoritarianisms in human history, when the support dwindled, we saw even the most fervent supporters attacking the actual oppressor, or at the very least getting out of the way from the mob's path in-route to overthrow the "dear leader." It is a good time to remind us all that the authoritarian is only as powerful as his or her supporters.

And let us realize that some people will be very convinced of whatever this authoritarian has to say. Evidence be damned, they will blindly follow this false doctrine to their last breath. We have seen people even committing suicide missions all over the world and throughout history based on a false belief. Interesting point, the authoritarian himself or herself tends to be very well protected while the followers put themselves in peril, every single time. And this peril could be physical or legal. That is why it is very inconvenient for an authoritarian or an authoritarian-wanna-be to have their followers enact critical thinking and intellectual honesty. If they did, these followers would likely figure out that they are being useful fools, and move on to do anything else other than following a crazy leader.

And crazies are abundant. You do not have to go too far to encounter this phenomenon. Any person with a platform, however big or small could potentially implant propaganda. How do you tell the difference? A propagandist will do "all the thinking for you" – they will "figure it out" in your behalf and give you the cliff notes. Normally this redacted narrative will be all positive for their dear leader, or even if the leader is not quite right, "there was a justification for their deeds." There is going to be passion, and there is going to be a "sense of confidence" – in fact, with the new media, there are probably going to be high-value graphics and production value to dazzle the followers into believing that a false narrative is legitimate. There are going to be talking points out of context, but they will not attack the <u>issue</u> on the merits. Instead, more than likely the charlatan will attack a <u>person</u> who is articulating those issues on the actual merits.

Facts on the other hand are impervious to emotion. The good, the bad, the ugly, the funny, the gaffes, the shortcomings, the percentage of correct/erroneous, the very long and boring unaltered sources of information, etc. All that and more will be available for you to see if it comes to describe a normal human being. The full context from either side good or bad is important to understand the full picture. That does not mean that a person despite seeing all the evidence will not make a wrong choice from time to time. But at least that way the person making this choice will OWN their wrong choice. When it is propaganda, consumers technically own their actions but we also have to understand that their choice was factored with faulty data. And the more naïve a person is, the more likely they are to become victims of a one-sided set of data. Yes, the data that seems to concur with their preconceived notions. In other words, their echo chamber.

But the authoritarian and propagandist already know what would set their followers into a frenzy. Some things will be prepped in a way that the obedient followers will give their very lives for their dear leader. And by the way, they would be giving their lives in vain. Yet, at the moment they would gladly fight to their last breath for a narrative they did not even really understand in full context. And yes, that happens a lot. And even if people are not killing in concurrence with a talking head, there is also many other forms of division. For example, people stop talking to their loved ones because the loved ones disagree on their devotion for a particular "dear leader."

Another example is falling into an echo chamber where only people with the same narrow level of misinformation seem to agree – while in their own minds they consider everybody outside that circle to be wrong.

Why do you think that happens? Well, if it was not obvious because of control. When you control the narrative and the amount of information your followers receive, then you can also implant emotions. These emotions do not need to brew instantly. Rather, plant the seeds and let it grow for a while. Artificially add another set of "values" being threatened by their perceived adversary and position these thoughts into a slow boiling frenzy. When the narrative is false, then the math is not going to add somewhere. Think about it like simple algebra. Let's use an illustrative equation as an example.

$$26(x+y)+(x+y-z) \ 4(z+y-x) = 95+\frac{(-z \ x)}{y-z \ (x+3)}$$

What is the value for "x?" what is the value for "y?" and the value for "z?" Spoiler alert, different values for each variable (x, y, z) might seem to fit the equation, but it will not quite resolve it. Do not worry, I don't expect you to actually use math to solve this sample equation. I just want to illustrate in a simplified mathematical expression how the authoritarian could be able to bamboozle people into a false narrative.

Using the algebraic expression let us say that the authoritarian will implant some statement of "truth" – but it will be redacted enough on their favor. Let's use these values for each variable:

"t" = Redacted Narrative - This will replace "x"
"f" = Statement of Fact - This will replace "y"
"u" = Leaving ambiguity - This will replace "z"

Then the authoritarian and propagandist (charlatan) will figure they can leave some things as true and some others out of context.

The original equation:

$$26(x+y)+(x+y-z)\ 4(z+y-x) = 95+\frac{(-z-x)}{y-z\ (x+3)}$$

Propaganda Narrative first step:

$$26(t+f)+(t+f-u)\ 4(u+f-t) = 95+\frac{(-u-t)}{f-u\ (t+3)}$$

Based on the authoritarian's evolving narrative as needed, the propagandist (charlatan) will start to emphasize certain points (**bolded variables**). These emphasized variables will make the story flow in a way that rallies their base strategically. Let us use the same equation as an example for how this might seem.

Propaganda Narrative emphasizing buzz points & rhetoric.

$$26(t+f)+(\mathbf{t}+f-\mathbf{u})\ 4(u+\mathbf{f}-\mathbf{t}) = 95+\frac{(-u-t)}{\mathbf{f}-\mathbf{u}\ (t+3)}$$

Of course that this equational example is only for illustration purposes. The actual equation for a narrative will be both a lot more complex, and there are millions of combinations based on the circumstances. That is why I said it can be very abstract. But if you look closely at the example, you'll notice that they will deploy a bit of manipulated truth along with the facts and leaving a lot of uncertainty. It is this uncertainty that can also create a visceral response on people. Much like a suspense novel, it keeps people in the edge of their seat so they can come back for more. And that is how facts have been taken over by "opinions" by large segments of the world population.

This sort of ambiguity is very convenient to the authoritarian, because there are going to point something they do not want *you* to see, because if you see them, then they will realize that some of the values in the variables they provided as empirical facts are in-fact erroneous.

When it comes to a person who is shedding light into the actual truth of the matter, the fact-checking will be able to show their analysis and assessment to disprove a falsehood. Let's use this designation to demonstrate this:

"a" = $\underline{A}$nalysis & $\underline{A}$ssessment - This will replace "t"

This replacement of "t" as the redacted narrative with "a" as the assessment & analysis of course will make it inconvenient to the propagandist. Because even though the "u" ambiguity will remain unknow, there are now more data points available to approach to an empirical reality. This empirical reality is not conducive for an authoritarian to control the masses.

Propaganda Narrative destroyed by analysis and assessments:

$$26(a+f)+(a+f-u)\ 4(u+f-a) = 95+\frac{(-u-a)}{f-u\ (a+3)}$$

Notice that if the propagandist already enhanced some talking points, then a proper assessment will not only destroy their narrative, but it could potentially sway the opinion towards their opposition's doctrines. In other words, the opposition will catch wind they have been bamboozled and would start questioning what else has been misconstrued, or downright false from the mouth of the authoritarian and their propagandists.

The next step for the propagandist (charlatan) will be to create division in any ambiguity. Either manipulate this data in a way that will regain the masses onto the side of the authoritarian, or downright negate the opportunity to have fact-checked information freely available. Let us use this to demonstrate this paradigm.

"c" = manipulate the argument by implanting $\underline{c}$onspiracy theories - This will replace "u" in the equation.

Propagandists will start throwing conspiracy theories to muddy any understanding of the facts, and analysis & assessments: Leaving ambiguity hidden within other values.

$$26(a+f)+(a+f-c)\ 4(c+f-a) = 95 + \frac{(-c-a)}{f-c\ (a+3)}$$

Notice that some of the boldened points were already part of the fabric of that society. Therefore there is going to be a lot more power to some conspiracy theories that will resonate with the more naïve segments of the society who will support the "dear leader" no matter what.

Some ambiguity will exist, because everybody has an opinion and information will be segmented. The complete truth is ever-out of reach to the general populace. At this stage it could go either way, because some people will cling onto any shred of concurrence with their narrow view; thus discrediting any of the actual facts and analysis & assessments. And by the way "a" (as in *one*) analysis & assessments could be work in progress, but currently trending in the direction of actually finding empirical data before they graduate to the level of "f" fact.

Well, at this point is when the "woke" or person with actual critical thinking and intellectually honesty can recognize the facts are not in the favor of the authoritarian, the propagandist, and their followers. Let us use this to demonstrate this next step in the process:

"k" = critical thinking & intellectual honesty - This will replace "c" in the equation.

People with critical thinking & intellectual honesty will be able to discredit conspiracy theories with statements that are actually logical, measurable, and demonstrable. In other words, they are not buying the bullshit conspiracy theories a charlatan will try to sell to them. This is inconvenient to the authoritarian & propagandist.

$$26(a+f)+(a+f-k)\ 4(k+f-a) = \frac{95+(-k-a)}{f-k\ (a+3)}$$

<------------------------ = ------------>

This side EQUALS this other side

When an equation gets solved, if the formula can be resolved from left to right, then it can be reversed engineered. If you cannot do this then something is missing. Those missing links will be happily filled by somebody who wants to control that narrative, and will prevent people from enacting critical thinking. Sure that doctrines will seem very different from one side to the other, and you might not have to agree in the way they reach the same conclusion, but at least you would understand the process. However, the more you understand the process, the lesser the chance for a charlatan to implant false narratives. Some of these narratives are disguised as buzz words that are designed to create a visceral response in order to divorce yourself from reality.

That is one of the reasons why you will see people who have something to lose embarking in a campaign to censor information. Or deny science, or negate any alternative ways to actually reach to the same conclusion from different sources that are not their "approved" world view. But beware, because this can be also weaponized by a shrewd propagandist to create a hyperbolic foe that does not exist, and rally people to support a non-sequitur.

And yes, that happens a lot. Part of the propagandist course of action is to create outrage and cover reality with opinions. There will be a lot of "what about-isms" and "so and so did this, therefore why can *they* do it but *we* cannot?" Expect this or a similar course of action anytime the charlatans can be proven to be at fault.

It is designed that way, to polarize people. Separate the loyal blind followers and everybody else who dissents. However, they will not tell you WHY they dissent, they will rather demonize them and paint them in a caricaturized manner in order to assassinate their character in the hopes you'll be distracted-enough to not pay attention to the fact they (the charlatans) are making you cling to a false narrative. They will not attack the issue; they will attack a specific person behind the issue. And you can be sure that if they paint them as "dumb" it is because these dissenters are anything but dumb, they are holding the key to get that "k" and "a" (critical thin<u>k</u>ing & intellectual honesty and <u>a</u>nalysis & <u>a</u>ssessments) in our illustrative sample equation. That is inconvenient to the charlatans.

Book burnings, anti-science rhetoric, "conveniently placed" conspiracy theories, punishment for dissenting with dogmas, prosecution of intellectuals, attacking educated people or those who seek education, tilting the opportunities to gain knowledge, call actual journalism "fake news," demonizing fact-checkers, giving "opinion" or "editorialized" content the same credence as actual factual journalism, posting derogatory or unflattering images of the opposition to discredit then under a false narrative rather than the actual merits, infiltrate peaceful protest with a few well-placed "vandals" to discredit a peaceful movement as violent, insult the disenfranchised if they plea for fair treatment, create paranoia that the other side is coming to get them, elevate tropes on any sort of discrimination towards others who are not considered peers in their version of society, dehumanizing others by depicting them as lesser human, use tactics of intimidation and calling others a derogatory epithet if they complain, etc. I can go on forever. But all these cited are examples that an authoritarian and propagandist will use (and have used in history) in order to incentive or even mobilize their followers.

And if you remember the previous chapter, I mentioned that people tend to seek "conflict" in order to remain engaged in a topic. I gave you the example of a movie with no conflict, and that it would likely be viewed by no-one. However any other movie with any sort of conflict would have a much higher degree of success - while the other alternative would be a snore-fest.

However, even in the movie with conflict the plot could turn into a snore-fest or an eye-rolling-time-parasite if there is not at least some sort of credence in order to make the movie even watchable. Sure, for some who do not know better a very half-baked plot will be enough to entertain them, and even enjoy it. But for others who have a higher level of understanding this same movie will be mediocre at best, or unwatchable at worst. Propaganda works in a similar way. It is a sinister art form, but it can backfire if it is not resonating with the population. And yes, at some point the allure will fall flat. That is not a matter of if but when.

This is important to understand early on in order to deny an authoritarian wanna-be the opportunity to galvanize their absolute power. Once they do it, violence and prosecution will follow. And yes, authoritarian regimes rig the laws in order to make it legal to prosecute people they do not like, even if it is otherwise considered a crime against humanity. We have countless examples of events like those in history and in contemporary circles. Yes, as I am writing this, there are no shortage of authoritarians-wanna be who are desperately rallying their next generation of followers, which in some instances become a political base.

The writing is on the wall, and the authoritarians wanna-be understand this dynamic very well. They do not want YOU to understand it, they will just tell you want you _need_ to hear. And if need be, they will explain it in ways that point their opposition as the roots of all evil. In political circles in the U.S. could be something Right vs. Left or Left vs. Right. The country is polarized already, that is already giving the authoritarian wanna-be even more power with minimal effort.

Let us take a moment to understand that part of the authoritarian & propagandist tactic is to infiltrate misinformation in a good cause to ridicule, or to muddy up the waters. If they are skilled enough, any valid dissenting doctrine will become a satire of itself and suffer a natural death. In other words, something gets so "uncool" that it falls out of favor from the general population. Yes, just like in marketing. A product could be superior, but lose the war in the consumer market.

Let me give you an illustrative example. The format wars. Back in the day Sony came up with the Betamax format. This was a video cassette for essentially very early home-entertainment systems (relatively speaking). Fast forward to today you can stream high quality content to your mobile device, or whatever other device you have. It was not like that even a few years ago. A Betamax was a video tape-player/recorder that would allow you to record your TV shows and play it back at your leisure, or even rent a movie and watch it in the comfort of your own home.

The movie studios at first were very much opposed to that, because that would mean that people might prefer to watch movies at home than pay a ticket to watch them in movie theaters. Also, people would no longer be subjected at the unlimited whims of a TV schedule to watch their TV shows. But with licensing's and other copyright punitive actions these big money content creators were able to somehow curtail it. And it worked, movie renting was big business. Soon enough, after Betamax was announced another competitor started to gain more traction. VHS, this was a larger format. The Betamax cassette was a bit smaller and a VHS cassette could hold a lot more run time because it was a larger cassette. Betamax had actually a higher video quality than VHS. But Sony made a huge mistake, they stubbornly only wanted Sony to sell Betamax to the world. VHS in the other hand licensed its product to a bunch of competing manufacturers. Betamax suffered a natural death because even though it was a superior format it lost favor to the general audience. VHS was able to capitalize in the fact that it had a larger following and it became the standard for home-video entertainment until the DVD came to the market.

Guess what VHS manufacturers did when that happened? They freaked out, and wanted to remain the format of choice, well they did not, but it took a while. Why? Because VHS would allow you to record your TV shows, while DVD only allowed you to play whatever was already recorded. And they were expensive. There were other short-lived formats in the market besides those formats I mentioned. For example, there was a CD-like format the size of an old LP vinyl record. It did not catch up because it was super expensive, and you had to flip it half way down the movie. Hence the DVD being the same size as the new Compact Disks for music was a more viable format. But as I said, you could not record on those disks yourself at the time. You had to buy them with a movie or whatever is it that they had recorded there from the factory.

Eventually, technology improved and you were be able to record in a DVD! The quality of the DVD was already far superior than VHS and even Betamax, even though it was very low resolution in comparison to what we enjoy today. But hey, it phased out VHS. Then what happened to DVDs? They exist still, but even with Blue Ray disks and the short-lived HD-DVD, the consumer format for home entertainment continued to morph. Today it is very likely that you stream video services on demand. No need to rewind or go to the video-rental-store to see if somebody has a copy of whatever you wanted to watch in stock.

Propaganda works the same way. An authoritarian and their rhetoric could be all the rage at some moment in time - that is not going to last. Somebody will be able to figure out something that was an unknown or had room for improvement and work on it. Obviously, that was not something that the established status quo wanted. It is obvious why. Because they would become a relic from the past. The difference with authoritarians is that they tend to do a lot of criminal activities. And if they fall out of favor, they often don't just get fired or broke, but rather could get prosecuted or brutally killed.

Now you can see why it is so inconvenient, and why they would cling to any shred of straw-man argument they can get. The real "woke" is the one who would <u>accelerate</u> their <u>inevitable</u> demise. Makes a lot more sense why they would demonize "woke" so avidly, huh?

CHAPTER 4

POLITICS & PROPAGANDA|
A Galvanizing Tool for Good and <u>not</u> Good

Politics and propaganda have been very much intertwined from the very start. *Does that mean that every politician is a producer and disseminator of propaganda? No, it does not. Although the more cynical would say it is rare if they aren't. There are some politicians who are honest and want to do the best for their constituents. That does not mean they are not going to make mistakes, even grave mistakes at some point. Nobody is perfect, and we all have blind spots. However, there is no shortage of cases of politicians who garnished power for the exact reason to enact a self-serving rhetoric. This is what I call the "authoritarians wanna-be" – there are many out there.*

Fortunately, most are not very good at it, and won't raise towards "full authoritarian" - but that does not negate the fact they could be extremely dangerous and damaging Some of these will be insider threats who are repeating foreign adversarial state-sponsored propaganda and adversarial talking points verbatim. It happens more often than you think. Some are perhaps doing wittingly with nefarious intent; others are probably too stupid to realize they are doing so. In other words, these useful fools could become puppets, wittingly or unwittingly from somebody pushing a narrative. They become pawns on the game, the problem with these pawns is that they have a following. And <u>that</u> captive audience is what the actual authoritarian and propagandists are going after.

For better or for worse some people fall victims of somebody who is better informed than they are. These are useful fools, and they tend to be very cynical and vocal about their misconceptions. Of course, they will talk about their misconceptions as empirical facts, even though they cannot demonstrate an actual viable shred of evidence to their claims, and they tend to talk themselves into corners when trying to articulate the points they repeat from their "dear leaders." And this repetition might be unknowable. That is why propaganda can be so effective on unsuspecting minds.

And there is a reason why they sound deluded. Because they are misinformed. The reality they consume is so skewed that the math does not add up, and they will have to make extreme mental gymnastics to put a world view under a very narrow lens. That is why when you try to argue with a person who has been compromised in that manner, they will get extremely defensive and irreverent.

It is borderline endearing if it was not actually so disturbing. And yes, it is very damaging, and it is very dangerous. Let us explore why.

This might come to a surprise to you. But when it comes to YOUR political leanings and principles, an authoritarian wanna-be does not care. It is more important for them to know what biases you have and how susceptible you are to exploitation. If you happen to lean towards the doctrines they claim to advocate about, great! They will feed you more information to demonize the other side until you become a very obedient and loyal follower of whatever is it that you are *supposed* to be against from now on. Never mind that if what you're against now it is something that was never a point of contention to you. As I said, your actual principles are irrelevant for this part of the process.

If you happen to be in the dissenting camp, something similar happens. There must be a bias or a vulnerability you have expressed at some point in your life, even if it was decades ago. They will find that and use it against you if you start to get too vocal against their narrative. Character assassination will be attempted or will occur well before your actual message comes out to a larger audience. But before the character assassination occurs, there will be some additional options.

Option number 1. Try to get you to fight on <u>their</u> side. They say through the grapevine that everybody has a price, and sometimes that price comes in the form of coercion. If you play ball for whatever reason, now they can get more dirt on you, or be able to use this as a leverage should you decide to stop playing ball.

Option number 2. Discredit you and demonize you. It does not even need to be a fair fight. Slandering, half-truths, and other demoralizing campaigns are often used. Also plant false evidence or try to use loopholes in a legal system to stop you on your tracks. This can also be used as political attacks, or even mobilizing a group of followers to intimidate (and in some cases harm) the person they dissent with. However, the later cannot be done until unilateral power has been established to "legalize" such an action – even if it is still a crime against humanity. But remember, the authoritarians will bend rules to make them work in their favor. This bending is just not sustainable.

Ok, so this is very scary, right? How can you stay above all of this? Well, mitigate any attacks to your persona are perhaps impossible one way or the other. But you are less likely to be coerced into any of these options if you're genuine and you stick to your principles without being nefarious to any other person. In other words do what is right as often as possible. If you make a mistake apologize and rectify it. Do not practice double standards, and if you learn something new that makes you a better person, then become a better person. We all have blind spots, we all make mistakes, we all have done something we are not proud of. But hopefully those lessons learned help us become a better person, even if the road to improvement was challenging.

The authoritarian wanna-be(s) portrait themselves as though they are never wrong. Or if they apologize, they will continue to commit the same fault over and over again. An apology followed up by repeating the same offense willingly is meaningless. And we have to realize that when it comes to politics, some people get elected to their seats with a lot of baggage. This is what it is known as "special interest groups." Some of these groups could include lobbyists, donors, other politicians, people with some sort of influence (e.g. oligarchs, organized crime, religious groups, extremists, etc.). And no, that is not only in the United States of America, this can and does happen around the world.

Some of these politicians are the "Option number 1" we were just talking about. I'll give you an example. And you can look at videos (if you search for them) from these political figures to confirm exactly what I am telling you to be factual.

And in case you did not realize it before, I will go out and say it. Some politicians will lie with a straight face for political gain, or to push an agenda. Yes, they will tell you one thing to your face, even if the cameras recorded and broadcasted their statement to the entire world, then they will do exactly the opposite of whatever they stated on camera. And then they would go on camera again and demonize something they advocated for before - when it was politically convenient for them. And yes, they often get away with it because normally their base, the people who vote for them, do not really care to remember whenever they were fighting for perhaps the very same principles they are now advocating for <u>or</u> against.

And that is what I was saying before, many followers are actually good and decent people who just happen to be making decisions based on a very controlled set of data points. Others, well, others are just simply assholes. The latter group very well know they are deceptive and they will do any mental gymnastics to prove they are right, even if they in essence <u>disagreed with themselves</u>. People like this have no principles, and really are just awful people. And yes, they exist, and they vote, and they are swindlers, grifters and drifters. And to add insult to injury, a lot of them have quite a platform. But make no mistake, due to the fact their entire premise is based on a lie, their agenda is not sustainable. They might enjoy a fun ride for a while, even decades, or even pass it from one generation to the next, but at some point, it will end.

And that is why I said it is very dangerous. A person does not need the spotlight for too long in order to damage something in a catastrophic manner. Think about it like a car accident. Your car is nice and shiny and it is super awesome. Then someday an asshole who has no business being on the road rams your car and destroys it the very few seconds they collide with your automobile. What is the aftermath due via this idiot ramming your vehicle? Well, it depends, but a host of damage can occur in those few seconds. It can range from a small scratch, to severe damage, injuries or even casualties. Same thing with these unsavory people who get elected to a position of prominence. It might seem like they have "business being on the road" but they are going to "ram" a bunch of people and destroy lives... sometimes for generations to come.

No, I am not being hyperbolic. This has happened throughout history. A person gets elected, maybe after many tries, or gets into power by force. Whatever the reason, if there are no checks and balances corruption will allow power to concentrate in a very small circle of cronies. And no, the majority of the "followers" who put them in that position will not benefit from this. They were never intended to benefit. The authoritarian wanna-be only needed them to get to the position he or she wants to climb to. After that, the authoritarian could not give a damn about what happens to their followers, unless he or she needs them to fight for him or her against the opposition.

Look at history, a lot of the worst authoritarians were pretty moderate at the onset, but then they started to move further and further to whatever side of authoritarianism they pursued. Unsurprisingly, when they were "moderate" (although leaning to either side) but largely unchecked, they rigged the laws into their favor. Once they did that, everything else became a lot more self-serving. They will then exploit their people, the opposition more harshly than the loyal followers to give them the illusion of being "on their side" – but they are all many notches below the authoritarian himself/herself. Subsequently, everybody becomes disposable, even the closest allies. If they become inconvenient, they will fall from grace immediately. And depending on the type of regime, often unceremoniously or even violently. I am not kidding, read history, this happens.

And it is happening in some countries around the world as you are reading my words.

Again, this is not a left or right side of politics. Authoritarians can and do come in either extreme. There have been terrible regimes from authoritarians that swung from extreme left to extreme right, and others that swung from extreme right to extreme left. And the reason for such an extreme swing it's because of radicalization. Even the mere fact of trying to combat an authoritarian can sprout other opportunistic leaders to swing the spectrum to the other side. History is peppered with examples like that.

An authoritarian wanna-be in a politician's role will first choose a side. Any dissenting side will be demonized, and if possible humiliated in any way. The lesser-acute-minds will actually rejoice in a low-blow, zinger, so called "owning" – (even if it was not really such a thing), insult, back-talking, talking-over, silencing, etc. from a perceived political dissenting figure. This figure could be a reporter, another politician, a private citizen, a person with an incumbent authority, etc. It really does not matter as much as the fact of whether it gets a catchy "sound bite" for the more naïve segment to claim that circus as a win.

It becomes kind of like a game. An opposing team, even if it is not a team you normally root for, but it is the opposing team for *this* game. This much like in sports can create a visceral response in people. People who are very impressionable tend to be very attracted to somebody who seems to be "in charge" – just because they use a certain stern tone, or sound like they mean business. Even though whatever it is coming out of their mounts is pure bullshit. And by bullshit I mean fearmongering, conjecture, whataboutisms, falsehoods, conspiracy theories, insults to the opposition, mocking the integrity of actual journalism, demonizing the opposition by clinging to some trope that will rally the base's biases, talking over "guests" they are supposed to debate, use anecdotal examples that are divorced from reality, use token dissenters from the opposition to invalidate a point, invite guests who are not at the same level of skill to debate a topic and "get owned" in a way to discredit their doctrines, etc.

I can go on for hours, but I am sure you have seen this with your own eyes, and maybe even been guilty of being happy when your side is "winning" without really understanding the actual context. Just remember that confidence does not always equals capability to perform at the appropriate level.

And if the latter is the case, do not beat yourself up. Own your mistake, and learn from it. If you are intellectually honest, then you will be able to take corrective action. And intellectual honesty is not being honest with somebody else. It is being honest with yourself! If you are honest with yourself, then it does not matter if somebody tries to discredit you, because you know that in the end facts are impervious to emotion. No matter how untrue a statement anybody utters, you will be in the right side of the argument.

Conversely, a person can be a lying sack of excrement, a grifter, conman or whatever. They might even get away with it in front of other naïve followers. But if you know you are a lying piece of crap, then you are in fact a very bad person and have no right to discredit others who are in-fact honest. You can attempt to hide the truth from anybody, but you cannot ultimately hide it from yourself. If you are a willful lying piece of crap because you choose to be dishonest, then that is reprehensible. What are you standing for? For a world of grifters? Are you thinking this is sustainable? What about the repercussions when it finally catches up with you? By the way, it is not sustainable.

Chances are that people who fall into that category would have an "I don't give an F-" to every question I asked. It is not surprising nor unexpected. These types of people become the perfect disposable obedient useful fools and errand boys and girls to the authoritarian wanna-be. The saddest part is because they are not honest with themselves, they are always slaves to a lie. And that is no way to live. It is a sad existence, and they have to live watching their backs. There is no merit, nor freedom on that, even if this deceit put them in a golden cage of their own making. Every swindle comes to an end sooner than later. And the punishment for those deeds far outright the shallow rewards they perceived to have.

Politicians have seen this happen over and over again. Lose an election, lose a race, and if they did some shady things the lawsuits and scandals will soon follow. And the controversy follows likely because there was evidence to prosecute, or at least to create a gigantic inconvenience. But that is why a lot of these unsavory personalities' acolytes will cling together in some shape or form. They tend to galvanize radicalized naïve followers who do not care about being honest, they care about "winning" – but what they don't realize is that "winning" with dishonesty its in-fact losing at a much larger scale.

In other words, even a small win, if not strategically viable will be a huge loss regardless. It might be a matter of time, but it will happen. And the way to know it will be strategically unsound is if it was based on a lie. Yes, even military operations. If it is based on faulty information the math is not going to add somewhere. It will fail. But if the strategy is based on facts and reality then it does not matter how complex it gets, all the pieces will automatically fall into place.

When something is based on a lie, then it does not matter how much you plan and refine the plan. There are always going to be glaring vulnerabilities and the chances that a simple statement could make the entire castle crumble to the ground.

The authoritarians and propagandists very well understand this (or at least come to realize it at some point), and that is why they will discredit anything that could potentially exacerbate that risk of their base finding out the actual truth. Politicians who lack scrupulous or wits will be perfect vehicles to spread this misinformation and even introduce it as legislation. Even if it does not pass as legislation, it at the very least buys more time to filibuster the process as the authoritarians and propagandists move the goal post. If you stop for a minute to think about it, you realize it is common sense. That is why some politicians will speak from both sides of their digestive track with a straight face.

But in order for this propaganda to take effect it needs naïve people who are receptive to this otherwise highly controlled misinformation. And quite the paradox occurs, the authoritarian and their propagandists will go in a counter campaign discredit actual facts as though those were propaganda points. And guess what? Naïve followers who are willfully or unwittingly ignorant to the context will eat every word spewed. They will even repeat the talking points. We will talk about that topic in detail in the next chapter. But remember, these talking points had to come from somewhere. And if you thought the corrupt politician is actually in charge of this narrative, then you have not been paying much attention to what I have been saying in this book. This world is very abstract, and it takes reading between the lines to find the context missing behind every phrase and sentence.

Corrupt politicians and propagandists want you ignorant and confused. They want you smart enough to repeat their propaganda points, but dumb enough not to understand the way they are pinning you against your own best interests. Again, this is not a left or right issue. Your political leanings are irrelevant in the great scheme of things. It is more important how naive and vulnerable to exploitation you allow yourself to be. Your support is only needed until you become inconvenient to them.

CHAPTER 5

USEFUL FOOLS|
Parroting Platitudes Without Context

If you are familiar with my writing then you know that I will cite the Dunning-Kruger effect quite often, and for good reason. If you have seen it before, you will see it again in this chapter, and it is worth repeating because explains why some people seem to overestimate their understanding on particular subjects. This affects the way people perceive the world, and can make them quite exploitable. How many times have you come across a person who spews information that is totally erroneous, but they do it with such confidence despite the facts to the contrary? It is possible to be long-winded and speak about statements of fact, if the facts are indeed real. However, it is also possible to be long-winded and ramble on platitudes that are divorced from reality. The authoritarian and propagandists (charlatans) prefer the latter. And these useful fools' ammunition will become talking points that lack context and substance. Even if they sound plausible given the very narrow of state of actual understanding. The propagandist wlll make it "easy enough" or "oversimplified" in a way that creates a visceral response. "Me good, they bad." Simple as that in concept, but quite a sinister art form in execution. Let us explore more.

If a complex issue seems too simplistic, then the math is likely not adding somewhere. For those in the echo chamber, this discrepancy in logic and substance will go right above their heads. They will repcat talking points that their favorite content creators have carefully, or in some cases arbitrarily crafted for them. Whatever the case, you can be sure that the entire story has not been afforded to the useful fools. The propagandist wants them stirred enough to pay attention and subsequently moving rhetoric into action at a convenient time for the propagandist.

This rhetoric will create a level of "trust" and "rapport" with the propagandist. Let us understand that if somebody is about to swindle you, the swindler is not going to tell you to your face they are about to make a fool out of you. Instead, they will make you feel like the smartest person in the room. Somehow, they seem as though they "can read your mind." They are not reading your mind, they identified your biases, and that is how they can exploit your underrated instincts. It is actually a disgusting thing to do onto others, but it happens all the time.

For anybody who is unfamiliar with platitudes, it means somebody is using "catchy phrases" or "cliché accounts" that could sound as though they could be related to an actual situation worthy of attention, but they are in fact not corelated. In other words it is spin. Somebody is trying to confuse their audience with something that is inaccurate at best, or a total falsehood at worst. Under this context, these platitudes tend to be paired with some sort of faux-outrage that gets people fired-up about something that is in fact a fantasy. And that is why it is so dangerous; because this faux-outrage will overwrite rationality, thus allowing the actual situation they should be outraged about move through with ease, or even unnoticed inside the echo chamber.

At the same time, who do you think realizes what it is actually going on? In essence everybody else outside that echo chamber who has been paying attention to that issue. But those in the echo chamber are either convinced of a falsehood or are deciding with faulty information. In either case it does not matter to them, because in the premise a visceral response was implanted. This does not need to be "instant gratification" – some of these visceral responses brew for years, and even decades. Especially if some of this outrage spans for a long time, there is a high possibility that those who are now fed propaganda will not even recall this was an "issue" to a particular dissenting group.

That is the reason why sometimes you do not hear about an issue, or a term for several years – until it is time to "remember" something that was "seeking retribution" of some kind. And keep this in mind, this situation can be enacted for either side of the argument. When tension is allowed to creep in - and sustain, the friction and resentment – it will continue to evolve until it reaches a point where the propagandist moves the rhetoric into a call for action. This could be exponentially damaging to the reasoning on the "other side" of the argument, because there is a possibility the charlatan's followers stopped looking for factual indicators long ago.

I have said it in a previous book, and articles I have written. An authoritarian (or a leader for that matter) is only as powerful as his or her followers. If there are no followers, there is no traction. And *followers* is a loaded term, because traction might not happen by the original voice of the man or woman who came up with the original idea. Instead, this idea could very well be carried over by proxy to a much wider audience.

Let me draw you a non-propagandistic parallel to give you an understanding of what I mean. David Bowie wrote the song "the man who sold the world" – phenomenal song on its own right. Did well on its time. However, fast forward to the 90's and the grunge band Nirvana during their MTV Unplugged version covered that very song. Chances are that most people are familiar with the Nirvana Unplugged version than the actual David Bowie studio session.

Another parallel example, Paul McCartney (from the Beatles) among the many songs he wrote, he released a song titled "Live and Let Die." Great example of musical mastery as most of his iconic music. However, fast forward also in the 90's and the rock band Guns n' Roses covered this song in their Use Your Illusion I album. Again, we do not always get to hear the original author, but somebody else will carry that message to a different or sometimes larger audience.

And of course, neither David Bowie, Nirvana, Paul McCartney, or Guns n' Roses are propagandists nor authoritarians. In fact, they are all phenomenal examples of musical talent. It might be hard to believe it, but not everybody has heard of them. I invite you to do so. Listen to the tracks I mentioned in your format of choice. You'll understand why I cited them as an example.

But going back into our topic. We have plenty of platforms available to disseminate information (and misinformation) to a very wide audience. It can be in person, or it can be broadcasted in one way or the other. It can be in writing, it can be auditory, it can be audiovisual, it can be long format (such as a book or film), or it can be as easy as a comic-strip cartoon, or even a meme. Examples to expand communication are prevalent, and that is why there are entire industries that specialize in disseminating messages to a larger audience.

And because there is a gigantic industry it is also a reason why veracity of information passed can be muddied up in the process. I have mentioned it before in my writings, but it is worth repeating. A lot of the information that you read every day as "news" in reality are "advertisements" – cleverly presented as studies, or other manners of presenting a product in order to increase a market segment of the population. Some of these adds will focus on very niche segments, some will be globalized, and everything in between. The point is that if you are seeing or reading anything, it is not by chance. Even the news need to be monetized somehow in order to continue operations.

In other words, it is not intrinsically a bad thing that there are business models based on the dissemination of information. Legitimate news sources and broadcasting need the income in order to function. For example in a radio station, you might be able to listen to the message "for free" – just by moving the radio dial. However, it cost a fortune to ensure that *free* message has reached *your* radio dial. The station, the antennas, the transmitters, the microphones, the rest of the audio equipment, the furniture on the studio, the electricity to run it all, etc. All that cost a lot of money, even if for whatever reason the actual radio personality behind the microphone would work for free. Spoiler alert, they do not work for free; nor should they.

The difference is when this system is abused, and instead of disseminating facts, it starts disseminating falsehoods or very redacted "truths" that are dressed up in a way that is solely convenient to a propagandist. Either way you see it, this propagandistic method is deceptive. However, some of these platforms can gain a very wide audience, and these loyal audience members could be incentivized to commit atrocities, if they believe that a false outrage would justify their actions.

Equally damaging it is the gaslighting when somebody is onto something that could shed light on the actual problem, and others try to discredit it without understanding the context. Which brings me to the Dunning-Krueger effect. In my other books I've written about it, but very quickly let me explain what it is.

Have you ever had to teach something to someone, and even before you can explain to them whatever is it that you try to teach them, they act as though they are masters on that subject? Yes, even though they are not savvy on that subject at all. Well, spoiler alert, we are all vulnerable to this situation if *in our minds* we are convinced that we fully understand something complex that might seem simple on the surface. Simply put, many things & subjects are a lot more complex than what meets the eye. And if we think something with a certain level of complexity is too easy, there is a possibility that we are missing the actual context.

The problem is that people who have marginal understanding of certain subjects tend to give opinions that are simply divorced from reality. Facts are impervious to emotion. Facts are logical, measurable, and demonstrable. If they cannot meet this criterion, they are conjecture. And in the latter is where most people who fall under the Dunning-Kruger effect seem to operate. And that is what I mean by people "yelling platitudes." They would only see the world from their own small world view, and negate the gigantic evidence that would disprove their bias and assumptions. Why?

Because people do not like to be wrong. Yes, paradoxically that simple! And yes, there is plenty of complexity behind this "not like to be wrong." And some will do gigantic mental gymnastics to ascertain that a faulty reality is the only empirical truth. It does not work that way in the real world. Everything has some level of complexity, and the more we learn about something, the more we realize there is so much more to learn about <u>that</u> something. A useful fool will believe they already mastered everything there is to know about a particular subject. That's a logical fallacy, everything, no matter how simple (especially if simple I would argue) has room for improvement.

Please find below the Dunning-Kruger effect chart to illustrate this process. This is the same graphic you will see in the other books where I have cited it.

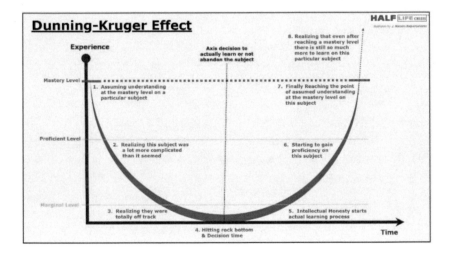

As you can see in the graphic, when people hit rock bottom, they can possibly gain intellectual honesty and critical thinking and actually learn the subject in question. However, at that critical vertices they could also simply give up, turn a blind eye, and delve into their echo chamber. And yes, that is exactly what happens to useful fools. And also yes, that is <u>exactly</u> what the propagandist and authoritarian are hoping the useful fools would do. To give up and just "go with the flow."

Sadly, as this phenomenon does happen at the macro level, it of course also occurs at the micro level. Sure, you might have your weird *uncle Timmy* yelling platitudes and distressing the family members during Thanksgiving; but in the higher offices around the world there are plenty of weird people like poor misinformed *uncle Timmy*. The difference is that in the higher offices these misinformed people have a lot more leverage and can create a lot more damage under their clout. These useful fools with a high platform tend to persuade a lot of other people who seem to agree with your crazy *uncle Timmy* about platitudes that are divorced from reality.

Do you know who benefits when that happens? No, it is not u*ncle Timmy*. It is not the person with the platform either. Though they might be getting a kickback of some kind. The one who wins is the <u>originator</u> of that misinformation. Keep in mind that if there is something that is put in front of your eyes, the person behind that narrative wanted to get your attention for some reason.

Some of us want your attention so you can realize what it is <u>actually</u> being put in front of your eyes. Others do not have your best interests in mind, and want to get you all spun up in order to push a rhetoric into action against a particular "enemy." This can very well be an "enemy you did not *know* existed," or perhaps this could be an exploitation of a bias you did have against a particular group of people. The difference is that a propagandist's end result is intended to disenfranchise those they want to oppress. And yes, sometimes those oppressed are their very own followers. Surprise!

CHAPTER 6

TARGETS OF OPPORTUNITY|
Taking Advantage of the Circumstances

Seneca said: " Luck is when preparation meets opportunity. "
The adversary has been preparing for a while. In some
instances even before you were born. Opportunists will come
and go, but the seeds of a greater narrative tend to permeate
through generations. The difference is that these might seem
dormant or even concealed from the majority's view. But for
those who know what to look for, they can find the vestigial
remains of an otherwise concealed narrative. These narratives
tend to be used as means to exploit a particular segment of the
population. Sometimes it is very subtle, sometimes it is
extremely violent and obvious. However, when something
complex (man-made or natural) occurs it did not occur by
chance. There was a series of events that were required
beforehand for that event or thing (whatever it is) in order to
be manifested. Those who are ready to act when this occurs
will have greater probability of success. Some others will die
without realizing what was underneath their very noses.

The circumstances in the fabric of society are dynamic.
Those who incorrectly think that the world is black and white
will be more prone to endure a rude awakening. Not a matter of
if but when. This awakening might not happen for years, or even
in *their* lifetime. However, these consequences could occur to
those they leave behind. Our actions will have repercussions.
Some will be positive and/or neutral, some will be negative.
Some of these repercussions will be immediate, some will take
a very long time to take effect.

Some of those repercussions might not affect <u>us</u> directly, but they will affect <u>somebody</u>. And those effects might range from negligible to tragic. For example, somebody shoots a gun on a public forest for "fun." Once that bullet leaves the gun's barrel it could simply hit a tree. But let us say that the bullet misses the tree and hits a hiker who just so happened to be walking about during their leisured day. Suddenly this action turned tragic. In theory it is tragic for both, it would be tragic obviously for the person who've got shot. Especially if this bullet impact causes severe bodily harm or death. And of course the person who owns this gun would be responsible for this projectile. Who is the victim? Of course the hiker who have gotten shot. The person who pulls the trigger in a firearm owns the responsibility for the round they fire, and the consequences for wherever this round impacts. But who suffers the most? The person who received the bullet wound.

And I know this story that might seem tangential to some. But consider that even though there are straight forward facts in that short example, this small narrative will open the door for a lot of misinformation. To make it contemporary with American political climate, there would be a rally in favor of the shooter from *some* pro-for-the second amendment folks. Some others will go on the opposite side of the argument and raise the concern about owning and operating firearms. However, the fact is that in this particular story somebody was reckless with a firearm and somebody else who was minding their own business got shot. Can it be called an accident? Perhaps, but remember that accidents are not necessarily analogous to negligence. So with this context, who is actually right in this argument?

Targets of opportunity will be similar in the sense that there will be a narrative and a set of facts. Some facts will be empirical, some will not be as clear cut. And the latter presents a ripe ground for misinformation. A shrewd propagandist would be able to weasel their way into the confusion. Any facts can be skewed if there is enough level of uncertainty in the context. And this level of uncertainty can be intrinsic or extrinsic. What do I mean by that? Willful ignorance and biases.

Targets of opportunity become more prevalent the moment the audience is ready to take information on face value, although vital context is missing. Especially if this vital context tends to be hidden in plain view or ignored outright. When people have a particular bias that is deemed exploitable, these are wonderful news for those who seek to manipulate this vulnerable crowd. The more a crowd is willing to ignore inconvenient facts, the easier they are to become subjects to manipulation. "Ignorance is bliss" is one of the most self-defeating defects a person could embrace. Seriously, it is very self-destructing.

We have all heard the old sage. "Those who fail to learn from history are doomed to repeat it." Yes, history has indeed repeated a few times. Some of the same techniques utilized by propagandists are not new. However, given enough time some old lessons tend to be forgotten by the newcomers. Sadly, also some people who were bamboozled before, could indeed be bamboozled again by a shrewd propagandist. Yes, with the same technique, although the scenario might be a bit different, just to provide enough contrast and let the willful ignorant follow their lead. Make no mistake, somebody wins on that situation. And no, it is not the vulnerable crowd of obedient willful ignorant people.

Society today is experiencing a paradoxically frustrating reality. There is literally gargantuan amounts of viable information at our fingertips, yet the level of willful ignorance is even greater. I remember when I was a kid, well before the internet was a thing, in our home we had several books and encyclopedias about many topics. Geography, history, literature, science, etc. I was lucky that my home was generally speaking inhabited by well-rounded adults who were able to instill on us some curiosity and the ability to open a book and learn on our own. I remember enjoying spending time reading and exploring all those many encyclopedias and literally hundreds of books in our home.

I would be remiss if I did not also point out that a lot of the information that we had available to us was in a way flawed. Although a lot of the encyclopedias were seemingly objective, once in a while there would be some bias depending on who was the author and the publisher. At the time we would not even think about this being an issue. If it was printed in a book, it should be true and good, correct? Well, apparently that assertion was not all-encompassing. Though most of the literature we had available at home seemed to be properly sourced and written, in hindsight I can see a lot of biases that were product of the times and the way the society instructed their citizens to follow.

Let me give you a few examples. There were some documentaries and even more books at my home that had some hints of either religious and/or political propaganda. Also, some of the scientific books, depending on the author were not as forthcoming as they should have been on narratives that were in contrast with reality. For example, some of these texts advocated for misogyny, gender roles, homophobia, antisemitism, falsehoods on historical events, etc. And yes, some of those did have a religious bias to justify these principles of discrimination. The saddest part is that people from all ages did not bat an eye when these narratives were percolated in our society. Afterall, it was *only* disenfranchising *other* people *outside* our group, *outside* our society.

That continues to this day. For some, these might seem like non-issues because it does not negatively affect *them* – those inside their own bubble. It affects *somebody else outside* this group. This fear about others without even knowing them is what makes us more prone to being manipulated into false narratives.

Whenever there is an "us-against-them narrative" always stop to think about who gets to benefit from that divisive situation? Spoiler alert, it will not be you who will ultimately benefit from this. If you get any benefit will be both incidental and temporary, only as long as the propagandist needs your support. For you see, as far as propagandists are concerned, the obedient and willful ignorant are just means to an end. I wish I could be less blunt, but the world we are living in is not going to care about your feelings. I do, and that is why I am being forthcoming with you. As you read my words, either you or somebody you love has been seduced by a narrative that is both divisive and is using you or them as a catalyst to support a narrative that is contrary to your actual best interests.

I mentioned earlier in this book, actual knowledge paired it critical thinking and intellectual honesty is inconvenient to a propagandist. The enemy will always be "lesser than the hero" in the eyes of whomever controls the narrative. This could very well be the truth, but it can also be a false narrative that is repeated over and over again to a crowd of people who will not do proper fact checking, hence won't realize they have been lied upon.

These liars are the opportunistic parasites who will exploit otherwise (often) good people into a narrative that dehumanizes their opposition. It does not matter how small or big this level of dehumanizing occurrences end up being; it can be as simple as instilling some sense of fear or "dislike them" without even knowing them. It is much easier to dislike somebody you do not know. When you get to know a person for who they really are, you might be surprised about how much you can learn from one another. Granted that not everybody is nice or even pleasant to be around, but you cannot determine that for sure unless you get a chance to hear from their mouth the rationale for their actions.

Let me give you an example, did you know that sometimes some very attractive people tend to be shy because they do not see themselves in the same light as others do? I find it fascinating that sometimes people who otherwise look like they have a permanent scowl are actually very nice people when you get to talk to them. I have met some people that just because they were attractive other people thought they were either conceited or even mean. Go figure, right? But once you get to talk to them, they might actually open up and really appreciate the fact that you can have a pleasant conversation, and you are not just approaching them because of their looks. And yes, this is actually from conversations I have had with attractive people before. Sometimes they even mentioned they kind of have that scowl because either some people treat them poorly or others are just hitting on them without actually caring to learn who they are as a person.

I personally treat everybody the same, no matter how "traditionally attractive" they might seem in their particular demographic. Why? Because they are people first, and everybody deserves respect no matter what they look like. Also, we must realize that attractiveness is also a very subjective view. Some people who are not "traditionally attractive" physically can be exceedingly attractive just by their charm and personality. And yes, this is true no matter their gender. In the end looks are temporary, but the essence of who we are will stand the test of time if we learn to appreciate ourselves for who we really are.

And I know that some of you might be wondering where I am going with all this? If it was not obvious enough, targets of opportunity at a human level are more vulnerable based on self-assurance and healthy self-esteem. You might or might not be surprised to learn that a lot of people with lower self-esteem tend to be very easily manipulated. This personal conundrum can be a treasure trove to an opportunist who is wanting to "help you find your way" at the expense of demonizing somebody else.

For example, without calling any region or country-against-country conflicts by name. Choose whichever country on this planet you want, these conflicts do exist and span all over the world, and they have existed from the beginning of human society. The rivalry can be between countries, between clans, between tribes, between ethnic groups, between cities, between political parties, between religious groups, etc. It does not matter – this "us against them" rhetoric is as old as humans walking the planet.

But for the sake of exactitude, let us take for example a very authoritarian regime (your choice). Are the people, the citizens living under that regime intrinsically bad? Or are they victims of a system that have entrapped them? True that some of their rhetoric and their world-view might be contrary to that of a different nation. But before we jump into conclusions you have to be objective about what type of environment are these citizens thriving upon. Who is controlling the narrative? Who is censoring the news? And more importantly, who is actually in charge of every thought and action these citizens are allowed to take? Are they in charge of their lives, or do they live in a place where there is "an illusion of choice?" Or do they live in a place where they are very well aware they have no choice at all?

For some of us in our cozy corners of the world, these levels of oppression might seem like a thing of fairy tales, or at the very least something that happens only to "somebody else." What people fail to realize is that those oppressed today were generally enjoying a lot more freedom before an authoritarian ascended to power. Moreover, many of these authoritarians who ascended to power were duly elected, and many of their followers rejoiced when they got into power. However, there were tell-tales signs already identified by those who understood what was laying *just behind* the "official" narrative that was approved for "all audiences."

Some of the most cynical would assert that anybody who gets into power could very well fit this criterion. And generally that is true, anybody who gets elected could very well seem as the "wrong choice" by their opposition. In fact, that would be commonsensical on the surface. But that is where the similarities end, there is a lot of subtexts that happens well before the elections even take place. For those who lack the context it will seem as though it is a very binary process. "I like this person to be the leader, I don't like this person to be the leader, choose it as such." Seems simple enough. It is not that simple, and that is why authoritarian regimes are able to thrive.

For people with an agenda, it does not matter what they tell you, it matters what they do, and what they have done. Talk is cheap, a politician or any other type of person in a "leadership position" can assert all kinds of tall-tales. Does that make their tales real? Extraordinary claims require extraordinary evidence. Promising something based on biases is an easy way to fire up a base of "loyalists" – but it is quite a different thing to bring that promise into fruition. Let us say for example that a person promises free housing for everybody in their party. Is that something that can happen? Technically yes, but the follow-up question is what is the standard for this housing?

Let me give you an example. Half-way through the Soviet Union history, the Soviet party was "housing everybody" in what the Soviet regime considered "adequate" quarters to the population. Was it adequate? Well, that depends on *your* definition of adequate. First off, people did not own property. They all had to pay rent, even though it was largely subsidized by the government. What some supporters of old Soviet rhetoric tend to fail to talk about when "defending" this *great idea* was for instance the details regarding the gargantuan waiting list for these "houses." Mostly really small apartments, and getting one of these dwellings was going to take several years. And also, these were so tiny that were not made for comfort but for very basic utility. People were not expected to live in comfort (compared to Western standards), that was a "decadent" lifestyle for only those "Western imperialists" who were living inside their "golden cages." However, the Soviet propaganda also showed as though the Western countries were living in destitution for the majority of the population who were not part of the elites. In other words, making this tiny apartment look like a luxury many Westerners could only dream of... in contrast to their own Soviet propaganda. How interesting, huh?

The Soviet propaganda would also show a lot of "success" stories and great "achievements" that were occurring somewhere else in the Soviet Union. And of course this narrative would present the premise that if everybody works hard and obediently as those other party members in other parts of the Soviet Republics, then the same level of achievement could be attained by those consumers of propaganda in this far corner of this similar, yet different Soviet Republic. Of course, that people in the cited "successful" community would be fed propaganda from a different "successful" community rather than their own. Bizarre, huh?

Well, the reality is that similar narratives happen around the world, and it is not only relegated to old Soviet propaganda. However, the principle is the same, divide people outside the circle of trust and control the narrative to those inside the circle of obedience. People in each circle are not necessarily allowed in both circles. It is very abstract for some people to grasp and that is why it is so effective. In fact, this level of propaganda is multidimensional, even if by chance.

When you see propaganda for what it is, and realize you are being lied to, it is very easy to understand the process behind the entire scheme. Much like when you learn the mechanics of a "magic trick." But for those who are immersed in propaganda, even if they are not the direct recipients from it, it can also create some interesting unintended consequences. Let us continue with the Soviet Union example to illustrate.

During the Cold War, the Soviet Union was gaining a lot of traction with some countries around the world. There was a very stark division of people for or against the Soviet Union. That was known as "First-World, Second-World and Third-World countries." Today when people think about First-World, they think some of the richer nations, and Third-World people think about the developing countries. But on the onset, it was a different dynamic, because the world was operating under a different dynamic, of course.

To clarify, essentially, First-World countries were nations that were aligned with the West and the U.S. Allies. Second-World countries were aligned with the Soviet Union and third world were not quite affiliated with any of the two former worlds, but depending on the regime they could swing from one extreme to the other. But remember, this First and Second World countries reaching to other countries was largely transactional, and it would also be based on a "need" that would yield a strategic advantage. That is why a lot of South American and African countries remained in the Third World. Neither the West nor the Soviets had a whole lot to gain about joining forces with many of those nations, unless these countries would align with their respective adversary AND had something of obvious value to offer to either the First of Second World.

For example, when Chile elected Salvador Allende – this new president was a Communist. The Soviets were happy about it; the Americans were not happy at all. And among other things this opened the door for Pinochet to eventually raise to power.

As a dictator, Pinochet was not a kind person at all, and under his regime a lot of people on the left-side of the political spectrum were brutally assassinated. However, Pinochet was against the Communists, so it kind of became a marriage of convenience for the First World.

And these marriages of convenience have occurred in politics from millennia. But more contemporary, in fact-leading to the Cold War. Before the Cold War era, the West – the United States of America and Great Britain became allies with the Soviets during World War II in order to fight the Nazis and the Fascists. We have to realize that things are a lot more complex than what meets the eye. That is why strategy tends to become closed guarded secrets in any government. Hindsight is always 20/20, but it is quite a different thing doing predictive analysis and nailing it. It is obviously not an easy task, and that is why when we learn history, we can see the many mistakes that governments from either side had made.

And some of those mistakes could otherwise be bad execution on well-intentioned expectations. Yet some of these good intentions can create severe unintended consequences that take decades for the aftermath to come to fruition. Continuing with this flip-flopping-relationship with the Soviet Union. After World War II, The United States went on the opposition to anything that was Soviet (you could argue for good reason). If they Soviets said "black" the United States would say "white;" if the Soviets said "party loyalty" the United States said "God" – and yes, there is a point to all this. And yes, this happened on the Soviet side as well.

Have you ever wondered where did the motto "In God We Trust" in our currency came from? That dates to 1955 when Dwight D. Eisenhower (Republican and deeply religious with Presbyterian denomination) was the President of the United States. It took two years after that time frame for these words to appear in the American currency. Well, the reason for this phrase in our money is not because the United States is a Cristian Nation. Despite anything you might have heard to the contrary, the United States Constitution in fact has an implied separation of church and state. Also, the Constitution does not specify *which* "God" is being trusted here. Presumably it is the God of the Bible, but it is not specifically implied. And yes, there are thousands of Gods in active and disbanded religions around the world, and many different "Gods" are worshiped even inside America.   But most Christians of course will take upon themselves to ascertain that it refers to *their* God. And in reality, those who advocated and prevailed to have it printed out in American currency where in fact followers of the Christian God, despite the fact that there is a constitutionally implied separation of church and state.

But yes, it was printed as a way to differentiate from people in the communist parties around the world. Many of which who were self-proclaimed non-religious. What some people fail to realize is that the established religions were outlawed by the Soviet Union because it threatened the authority of the Soviet party. Simple as that, not because people did not believe or even subscribed to a deity of their choice. In fact, did you know that Stalin actually attended seminar school? Yes, and he was quite adept to it also. But as with any of these corrupt politicians, the Soviet party became the de-facto deity. And the party demanded outmost obedience. It took the place of their "God" – but that does not mean that there were not devoted religious people in the Soviet Republics. Yes, some Soviets even worshiped the same Christian God from their Western counterparts.

In fact, the zero tolerance for religious doctrines had to cool-off after a few years particularly in the Asian countries in the Soviet Republics that were more closely aligned with Islam. The Soviets realized that if they had some "tolerance" of some religions, they were able to get more control over the population, rather than risk a religious war in some of the Republics. Religion is a very powerful catalyst for people's actions. The Soviets realized it early enough, and were able to manipulate this faith-devotion whenever it was convenient. For anybody else, if not deemed convenient for the regime, then the zero religious tolerance would prevail. Of course that traveling in the Soviet Union was very controlled and very hard for an every-day citizen to learn the truth, therefore most people would have never known what really happened in a different Soviet Republic. However they were all very well aware of the punishment for dissent.

And this unintended consequence for ultra-religiosity in the United States gained a lot of traction because they were fighting Communists ideologies at the time. This was also possible because the traction that religion had back then was very different than in today's society. In case you were not aware, religious affiliation (any religion) is in rapid decline around the world. Yet, this same faith-based "mechanism of defense" is now being weaponized in a way to divide the west. Those otherwise wholesome religious doctrines morphed into avenues for extremism. And yes, it did open the door for some opportunistic religious leaders. I am not saying that every religious group is extremist, what I am saying is that religion can very well be used to sway people into extremism. All these followers need to do is believe that *their* religion is the only correct one.

And that begs the question, which religion is the correct one? Yours? What makes yours unique? Because you feel it in your heart? Yeah, everybody else will assert the same thing. Food for thought. And the point here is not to divorce you from your faith, but to simply illustrate that if you felt even slightly uncomfortable by the mere fact that I brought that up as an interrogative, then *you* are also susceptible for manipulation under religious bias. Mind blown!

I wrote an entire book about religion and lack thereof; therefore I will not go into detail here. But I just wanted to show you that there are visceral emotions attached to religion, that is why I revisited it in this chapter. I can describe a lot of things as far as examples for religious biases; but to really drive the point, I need you to feel it and afford you the opportunity to see it from various sides in the event you're indeed vulnerable to that level of manipulation.

And if you are in the United States, please understand that a lot of that religious fervor that exists today was exacerbated by the paranoia that occurred during the Cold War. There was a very real threat of mutual destruction, and it was easier to bring people together as a "war between good and evil." Not surprisingly, a lot of new denominations sprouted all over the country. And no, most of those denominations do not agree with a large swath of their own doctrines. That is a win to the adversary, because unfortunately although these doctrines create a sense of community for their congregation, they are also divisive by nature to those outside the same.

Meanwhile, other points of view were highjacked in a way to create more division. Another example is the Second Amendment in the United States of America. Nobody is better at killing other innocent Americans than Americans themselves. If you live in the United Sates of America look to your left or right and somebody near you is packing heat. They may think they are the "good guy or gal with a gun." But how do you know for sure? So what do Americans do? Buy more guns and even give them as gifts to their children. Tools specifically designed to cause another human being bodily damage or death with ease are largely bought and sold mostly unregulated in the United States. Who do you think wins with all this? People who want to divide us. And they are achieving their goals in stellar fashion. Every other day there is another mass shooting in this country, and many politicians only offer "thoughts and prayers" – but I will go in a limb to say that thoughts and prayers have not fixed the problem of mass shootings in America. If thoughts and prayers were the answer, this would have been resolved many years ago. It has not.

By the way, this problem will not be fixed anytime soon at the time I am writing this manuscript. Why? Because there are a lot of political baggage and opportunism on that Second Amendment topic for and against this matter. But guess who praises the United States for standing tall defending their unregulated weapons when people get slaughtered in mass shootings every other day? All the nations and regimes who do not like the United States of course. Surprise! The difference is that a lot of American citizens quite frankly do not care about what is going on around the rest of the world, or don't really care to learn about it - if it is not affecting them directly. That does not make them bad people. Americans, just like citizens of any other country are product of their immediate environment.

A quick self-test to illustrate this point. Where was the country of Zaire located? And follow up question, where they friendly or unfriendly to the United States? Take a moment before reading the next paragraph. If you know the answer great! If you don't, just ponder for a bit. 10, 9, 8, 7, 6, 5, 4, 3, 2, 1.

Zaire is present day Democratic Republic of Congo; it is in Africa somewhere near the center mass of the continent. They were both friendly and unfriendly to the U.S. even though they had a terrible dictator because they had some interesting natural resources and some politicians at the time were okay "looking the other way." Now you know. But the larger point is that alliances or agreements with other governments happen all the time, and some do well and endure – others are not quite ideal, but strategically it is considered the lesser evil.

We have to realize that the world is not all roses and lullabies. I can understand why most people will prefer to be willfully ignorant to these atrocities. And in reality, when you understand the intricacies of the world it can be quite depressing. But just like adulting, sometimes you cannot change the circumstances in front of you. Blissful and willful ignorance is tacit consent for somebody else to take control over your life – or continuing taking control over your life with impunity. You might not even realize that is the case because this could very well be happening by proxy. But it is happening.

Those who realize it and raise awareness will not gain a fan club from the segment that is trying to oppress everybody else. There is a highly lucrative marketing in fear and in opportunism. If there is a visceral response you will be hard pressed not to see somebody who already made t-shirts and other merchandise "reading your mind" on exactly how *you* feel. Why do you think that is happening? Because it is part of the script. Some will pick up on the opportunism and create all kinds of money-making schemes to capitalize on that faux-outrage.

For example, have you met people who are very keenly aligning themselves with the "wrong side of the argument" on purpose? That happens all the time. This might be a token person who is a "dissenting voice" overtly against their own demographic. Why? Because controversy sells. And sadly, there are a lot of less-than-informed people who will follow a charlatan's non-sequiturs as though they are spot-on their assessments. But of course their assessments and rhetoric cannot meet even an inch-deep level of scrutiny. If they get cornered, they will become defensive, dismissive, or even mocking the people who know what they are talking about in an effort to discredit them. People like this exist, and they have no problem defending a position that is indefensible because of their search for notoriety (in their minds) helps them fill that lack of substance.

It takes a lot more courage to accept that there is a lot we do not know, but that also means we should also be taking the correct steps to learn as many true things as possible. Furthermore, it is easy to buy into a false narrative. The false narratives are designed to be easily digestible. Things that are erroneous will often be oversimplified for the masses. Things that are indeed complex will be as complex as they should be, but it will not be artificially inflated or overengineered.

What do I mean by this? If *something* is true, there is going to be a lot to learn about that *something*, even if it seems simple. If it is true, all pieces of the puzzle, no matter how you approach it are going to come together. Whereas if something is false, the math is not going to add somewhere, no matter how hard they try to make this falsehood as close as possible to reality. A falsehood will have a blind spot somewhere. Is that simple in the complexity. I realized I've repeated this before in this book (often), but it is worth mentioning again because I want you to remember it. Especially as we dissect each part of the process.

You will be able to realize that if somebody is using you as a target of opportunity their math will not add up. Somewhere in the premise or the execution there will be glaring discrepancies. If somebody is not fighting you in the merits but rather using a "what-about [insert distraction of choice]?" or other conjecture – then you can be sure they are in the wrong side of the aisle. Then the question becomes; will you place yourself willfully the wrong side of the aisle? Or decide to remain willfully in the wrong side of the aisle when you know better?

CHAPTER 7

INTELLECTUAL HONESTY|
There is a Complex World Out There

Critical thinking must be accompanied with intellectual honesty in order to be effective. Surprise! A person can have critical thinking and still remain stupid. Critical thinking without intellectual honesty only yields a parroting obedient fool. And these fools abound, some are in very prominent positions of influence (ranging from the micro to the macro level). That is actually a very scary thing because the dumbing-down of our society is happening at an accelerated rate. People who are in placed in a position of prominence who are not suited for that role contribute to the dumbing of the population. I cannot be kind about this, there are a lot of very ignorant people who have tons of obedient followers, and these followers are parroting otherwise demonstrably debunked points. It is important to realize that knowledge and understanding are not synonymous, instead they are complementary to one another. Knowing that something exists does not automatically means that we understand it. Many people know that quantum physics exists, a lot fewer actually understand it. There is a reason for that.

The most viable way to move forward in our life is by becoming better than the person we were yesterday. All of us have a path to follow, our path is unique. As long as you are better than the person you were yesterday you will be growing. People tend to forget that we cannot live from previous successes alone. Every day we need to move forward and become better. For example, if you ate yesterday – it is not a matter of if but when you will need to eat again.

If you slept yesterday, that does not mean that you will not need to sleep ever again in order to survive. Same thing with everything we do in our lives. What we accomplished yesterday is part of our history and our legacy. However, we can always accomplish something new. Even if you cannot replicate something you were able to accomplish in the past. But there will be *something* you will be able to do each day that will make you better than yesterday. For example, learn a new word every day, or learn a new topic you find interesting.

Another more illustrative example, if you climbed Mount Everest, you might or might not ever want to do that ever again, but you do not *have* to climb Everest again either. In fact, it might be as easy as talking about your experience to an audience you've haven't addressed before. Then your legacy continues and it will benefit the next generation without you having to climb again. Unless you actually want to or can climb again. That's a win-win.

And of course I chose a very stark example because it makes it easier to illustrate. But for most of us who will not ever attempt to climb Mount Everest (I know for a fact I have zero interest on climbing Everest), there will be something that we are in-fact interested in accomplishing. What I find interesting might feel like a boring situation to somebody else. Or maybe what I find boring is fascinating to other people.

That is the beauty of it, we can find our own path. The sad part in society is that a lot of people spend money they do not have on things they do not need to impress people they do not even like. I was one of those people at some point in my life, and it was very liberating breaking free from that unfulfilling trend. Today, I really only want to impress my wife and daughter… and they already love me and accept me for who I am – even with all my many idiosyncrasies. So I am good, anybody else who like me for who I am, that's just groovy but not required for me to feel happy. The happiest times for me are when I am with my two girls. Every other time might be memorable, but it will always take second place. I am sure that every person will have a different way to see the world. And that is their choice and their right. If they are happy, I am happy for them.

I should caveat with the fact that whatever we do for ourselves does not mean that we are *entitled* to do the same to other people. Yes, even nice things. It still needs the other person's consent in order to enact that action onto them.

Let me give you an example. Let us say that a person loves drinking coffee first thing every morning. The person likes it so much that he (let us say it is a dude) works it out with the bosses and subsequently makes it mandatory for the entire staff to make coffee every morning as soon the first person arrives to the office. There is a catch, this is the only person who *really* likes coffee, most everybody else likes tea, or do not drink either tea or coffee. What should be the resolution for this situation?

Well, it should be simple enough. The coffee drinker should be able to make his own damned coffee if he so desires. But what if the regulation is authoritarian in nature, and now everybody, regardless if they are a coffee drinker or not are *required* to make coffee every day if they are the first ones to arrive? What do you think it is going to happen next?

If you guessed that most of the staff will just wait until this coffee drinker arrives first to make his own damned coffee, you might be right. However, what if this person is arriving to work too close to the time where others would be tardy? The level of inconvenience to everybody because of somebody's "convenience" becomes an unbearable situation to the collective. In a similar manner (outside this simplified hypothetical example) the will of somebody who only thinks about himself or herself will negatively affect the collective.

Here lies the crux of this situation. Generally speaking, certain people who are socially inept tend to see the world from a very narrow scope. In *their* mind, they do not care how it affects others. For them *their* world view will generally be a "*me* statement" - and only become important to them if whatever is it that is happening affects them directly. As far as actually bearing consequences.

This is more common than you can imagine. Not everybody has an altruistic-driven personality. And by this, I do not mean that a person should be forced to be contributing to charity or volunteering time at a local shelter. In fact, and surprisingly enough to some, these socially inept people might very well be volunteering and even contributing to charity. Yet, they are very much dumb as rocks when it comes to understand how their behavior inconveniences the rest of the people around them. This has a lot to do with projection, and a sense of entitlement.

Unsurprisingly, people who ascend to a certain level of hierarchy tend to believe everybody else is *inferior* in the lower hierarchical echelons. Often forgetting what it was like when they were in said echelons. Some people might have never even experienced a "lower" echelon because they just so happened to be born on a "higher" echelon by chance. For example, parents who were very wealthy are more likely to give opportunities to their children. These same opportunities would be either out of reach, or would take a significant more effort for others in a lower echelon to even reach the baseline.

For instance, let us say that there are two families. One is an upper middle-class family and the other is a very humble working-class family. The same year both families welcome a child to the world. For this story they are both girls. Born the same day, same city. But that is where the similarities end. The upper middle-class family had insurance and the child was born in the hospital with all medical care. The family welcomes their child to the world and take her home to a beautiful nursery where all the toys, baby monitors, blankets, and gifts for the little one are already staged for her arrival. The working-class family did not have insurance, and the baby although born healthy will not be arriving to a brand-new home. For starters, the working-class family will be paying out of pocket for maternity-delivery-expenses for several years at a high interest rate. The toys and little room for the new baby girl is modest, and most are hand-me-downs, but the parents welcome her with love and make sure that she has the best upbringing they can afford to give her.

Fast forward, and both baby girls grown in loving homes. Both baby girls end up going to the same public school. They both are good students, but only one of them is able to afford the time and the expenses for additional extracurricular activities. Come to their teenage years, the upper middle-class girl gets a new car for her sweet sixteen, while the working-class girl has to work part time in order to help with expenses at home. This means that the working-class girl cannot afford to have "fun" with kids her age in the same fashion because of the life-responsibilities she has. The upper-middle class girl has the "choice" to work, but that is only as an incentive for her to develop professionally. Notice, for one of them is a need, for the other is a choice.

They both graduate. The upper middle-class girl has a fund to pay for college and has no student debt. The working-class girl was able to get a scholarship to pay part of her studies, but she still needs to get a student loan to cover the rest of the tuition. They end up graduating with the same degree from the same College. They end up getting the same type of job with the same salary in different companies. Are they in the same footing yet? Not yet. The working-class girl still needs to repay the student loan with the high interest before she can finally start reaping the benefits of her life-long efforts.

Does that make the upper-middle-class girl any less meritorious? Absolutely not. The young girl was a good student, she chose to work, and nowhere in the story did I say that she was unkind to the other young lady. For all we know they might or might not have become friends at some point. But the point is that they both have a very different baseline from the very start of their lives. Even before they were born. We are all given a different path, and we have to make the best of each situation. However, if somebody is asking for help when they already have a disadvantage, that should not be denied to them.

The reason why I framed this story in this manner is because I often read the posts from confused people who do not understand the fact that we all have a very different starting point. It is easy to see the world through a very narrow frame.

It is easy not stopping to think about all the thousands of factors that affect other people who do not affect <u>us</u> directly.

There is a sense of selfishness, sometimes unwitting selfishness which affect us all. Sometimes because we do not know any better. And in reality, it might be by design and with good reason. For example, I do not want my daughter to know what it is like to live in a household where there is alcoholism and violent fights as a routine occurrence. In-fact in our household there is no alcoholism nor violence. I also do not want her to have to deal with unpleasant and dangerous individuals who would dehumanize her in any way. Therefore I ensure that I can give her a stable home with loving parents and afford her a lifestyle where she can capitalize on her intrinsic strengths. That is very similar to my own upbringing. I had a safe and fulfilling life growing up. Hence my duty as a father is to make it even better for my daughter. In other words raise the standard as much as I can afford to do it.

Will I add some controlled learning objectives along the way in order to make her resilient and better prepared for the future? Yes, absolutely! But that does not mean that I will put her in a dangerous situation for the sake of pushing her off her comfort zone. I do push my daughter out of her comfort zone in a controlled manner, and that is working well, because she learns the lessons and is able to grow accordingly. As a responsible parent I do whatever I can to afford her that growth opportunity.

However, what I cannot do is for example sending her to a boarding school (not that I would do that anyway, I already feel like I do not get to spend enough time with her because of all the time I am floating on this ship). This makes me realize the obvious, every second is precious. And the way I choose to raise my child is perhaps not the way other parents want to raise theirs. In either case, I also have to ensure that as I raise my child, she also learns about having agency over her life, and that includes understanding consent.

My daughter, like any other child has her strengths and her areas for improvement. As a parent, I have to ensure I can identify and maximize the options presented onto us. And part of developing her agency and understanding consent is intellectual honesty.

When a person has intellectual honesty, then they are able to see the world from their perspective and understand how this perspective is being perceived from a different point of view. The result is empathy. At this point we can still decide if we will assist or leave something as it is presented to us, but at least we will understand the context for that situation.

To better illustrate this point, let us talk about the student loans situation in USA. I have seen these memes of people with a stern look pointing to an easel which reads "you took a loan, you repay it" – (no duh!) But this repayment situation is not as black and white. What some people fail to realize is that that loan principal amount ballooned due to interest rates, largely unregulated. Some cynical people will say that "they (the borrowers) should have not chosen a "liberal arts" degree for a career then." Which is a propaganda point by the way. Besides surprise-surprise some of those liberal arts careers make more money than other actual "careers" in a saturated market. Influencers taking photos of their meals, anyone?

For example, there are people with medical or law degrees who are flipping burgers because the saturation of the market where they are currently at. Also, even if they work at a hospital or a law firm their salary is eaten away by the student loans after graduation paired with the high cost of living (including the dwellings). So yes, they are working full time in their degree and flipping burgers to compensate their income.

We have to realize that the home-economics for a middle-class person is already very fragile. A bad accident, a bad injury, a broken appliance, a car repair, a death in the family, even a mild-accident, an unexpected bill, a sudden change in the property value affecting their escrow payments, a sudden lay-off from work, a natural disaster, etc. Any of those can derail an otherwise stable family who has been doing "all the right things" in a matter of minutes, even if this stability was years in the making.

There is also a big elephant in the room. There is such a thing as discrimination around the world, and yes, sadly that also includes the United States of America. Racism, homophobia, antisemitism, sexism, anti-science, etc. These are catalysts that create division between our people. We can very well measure these tactics from adversarial regimes. What makes the United States of America great is the actual diversity in the country. Sure that some very racists or otherwise bigoted people will advocate for the contrary, but what they do not realize is that they are repeating adversarial talking points that want us to be more vulnerable. In every major conflict where USA prevailed; it was because people from all walks of life worked together to make a better future for us all. When we underestimated our opponents, the conflict did not go well at all. But that is a different topic altogether. Back onto the more positive examples of American major conflict successes.

For example, during World War II, the Navajo Code Talkers. These were 29 people from the Navajo tribe who were originally selected to serve in the U.S. Marine Corps to develop a code to be used in battle. Their language is very complex but it did not have a written alphabet which made it ideal for coding; as a result the enemy could not decipher what they were saying. These brave Marines were able to rely orders over unsecure nets to other posts and accounted for very significant tactical and operational successes. During the war there were between 375 and 420 Navajos who severed as code talkers. The sad part is that despite these Marines being such an asset to the U.S., they were still discriminated against by some of the very people who wore the same military uniform – simply because their skin color was different. Also, the program was classified for a long time, and that is yet another reason why they did not receive the welcoming praise other units received after the war. But even after their involvement got declassified, it took a long time for these heroes to be recognized for their valor and extraordinary contributions in battle. There is plenty more to talk about this, but I wanted to cite it as another significant example of how history can be eye opening when we step off our own bubbles.

Similarly, the difference between segments of the population was evident during the Jim Crow era. Black Americans were discriminated against because of the color of their skin. And even though there were naval regulations that were *technically* against discriminating them, the reality on the ground was very different. The very type of jobs available to them was very limited and often relegated to what many would have considered "lesser" than their counterparts.

Even well after the times of segregation were no longer the law of the land, opportunities for black Americans remained out of reach for so many people. This is because of a systematic effort to keep them down since before the times of the American Civil War. You don't have to like my words; history played out the way it did. All this happened, pretending it did not is simply willful ignorance. I've said it before and it is worth repeating. YOU are not responsible for what your ancestors did during their time. But you are very much responsible for what you do today.

This is not the same as what the propagandists call "critical race theory" – this is history, period. Groups of people from all walks of life and skin colors have done great and terrible things throughout history. These are facts. Some people learned from those unsavory times and became better, and further learned about their shortcomings as to not repeat a bad chapter in history. Others simply tried to bury the truth and either unintentionally or willfully repeated it, or were otherwise somehow instrumental in repeating unsavory parts of our history. But make no mistake, unfortunately hate for others who look different or have a different skin color does happen around the world to this day.

Many of us, and we are the majority, fortunately… we realize that all people are people. We are all human. We all have red blood; we all belong to the same species. We are all unique and the same simultaneously. We all deserve the same rights as everybody else. To live and be happy. But our rights end where the other person right begin. You probably have heard this example before. I can swing my fists all I want, but my right to do so end if I am within a striking distance from anybody else. It should be very simple to understand, but this principle seems lost in a lot of people who choose to impose their views and doctrines onto others.

And this imposing of doctrines is where the waters tend to muddy up. In other words, some people might not even realize that they are imposing their will or doctrines onto others. And this happens to be part of the fabric of societies where a group is afforded a different level of privilege than another segment of the population they deemed "inferior" – and "inferior" is a very loaded term because it can come in more forms than people realize. Let us explore a few variants.

First and foremost it can have a hierarchical bias. Some people because they have attained or in cases inherited a certain level of privileged position automatically assume this endows them with power over other people. For example, back in the day when monarchs were born into nobility, the subjects were in for either a bad situation, or perhaps have a good king or queen every now and then. But if you studied history, you would know that a lot of kings and queens had the propensity for being very unpleasant people. However, if a person happen to be born in a less-than-privileged family, well sad day for them, their lives were going to be full of inequality and tribulations. And if they did not like it, well sad day again. Some of those monarchs would severely punish or kill their subjects for daring to ask for fairness.

Well, even though monarchies do exist around the world and some have more or less power than others. Still in those instances there are also people of "nobility" and they are also capable of being less-than-nice to people who are not considered of "noble blood." Yeah, it is not like you can go out and rub elbows with nobility in monarchies if you are a "regular" person even today, unless you have certain placement and access to be even in the mere presence of these people who happened to be born into nobility. This exists to this day in many different facets that are also not linked to nobility, but rather on position and authority.

In today's U.S. Navy we teach leaders that they must <u>earn</u> their rank <u>every</u> <u>day</u>. A person in the U.S. Navy could start from the lowest enlisted rank and make it all the way to the highest officer rank based on merits and other opportunities. Does that mean that everybody wants to climb the ranks to that position? No it does not. Not even every Junior Officer is interested in becoming a Flag Officer, or even a Senior Officer. We have that choice in the U.S. Navy because the United States of America is a free country. People choose career paths based on becoming the person they are meant to be, and both Enlisted and Officer career paths can be extremely fulfilling and unique in their scope.

Some people might think that attaining a high-rank means *that* should be the ultimate goal... but it is not. Each career path is unique and Sailors serve and leave the service after reaching one of the many ranks available to them. There is no problem with that, serving honorably for a few years or for an entire career is a choice, and the more merit a person accrues the more choices they are afforded under naval doctrine.

It was not like that way back in the day. People were relegated to a position based on their family heritage. Very unlikely that a run-of-the-mill person would be able to serve as an Officer back in the day. Today Enlisted people might get a chance to become Officers if they wish to pursue the requirements for that position. If they don't it is fine, because every career path has a high degree of intrinsic complexity. In fact, there have been cases of people who pursued a career from Enlisted to Officer and once they got commissioned as an Officer, they did not really like it too much and missed their Enlisted position. Others liked being an Officer better than being Enlisted.

Personally, I chose to remain a Senior Enlisted. And although I had an opportunity to become an Officer, I like more what I get to do in the position that I have for multiple personal reasons. In a separated manuscript I go in depth about all that.

Would some people out there think of Enlisted people as lesser than Officers because they do not hold the same rank? Yes, absolutely. Are they wrong, yes again, absolutely. You see, it is easy to misconstrued a trope because of a lack of understanding on the ground truth. I have heard as much before even in my own life. But when a person is self-assured and understands the intricacies of what takes to be in the position that we are, then the misconstructions of nay-sayers have little to no effect in the way we view ourselves.

When we see this in a macro projection and throughout history and present day, then we will realize what some people erroneously think. They *think* they are automatically better than others because they just so happen to have something that seems like a privileged position.

For example, they happened to be born in a particular country. Maybe they inherited a title of nobility due to their family heritage. Some are even convinced that the color of their skin makes them superior to others. And no, not only white people in history ascertained superiority to others because of the color of their skin. This shortsighted misconception over skin color happens even among people with the same skin tone. However, they might then further divide people based on "social class systems."

Let me give you a historical example. When the Spanish Conquistadores arrived to the "New World" - they brought with them also a very despicable social-class system. Unsurprisingly, if you were a European-born in Europe, you were considered the highest social class. If you were born in the New World, even though both your parents were born in Europe, your social class was already lower than of those born in Europe. And guess what? Europe was not always quite a phenomenal place to live in either. Ever heard of the black plague and the dark ages? However, they ascertained that this "birth right" automatically made them superior to people who were born in the American continent (the American continent is a lot bigger than just the United States of America, by the way).

Did some of these Europeans had anything that made them intrinsically more special than people in the New World? Not really, some of them were pretty ignorant and analphabet. Yet, they had an opportunity to go to the New World and "discover new lands" – lands that by the way were populated for several centuries before the Europeans ever set foot in the Americas.

This is part of what we see even to this day. Even during "biblical" times, people tended to subjugate other groups that were outside their community. And even outside biblical allegories different tribes and groups of people would fight with one another because they were considered "different." Especially if these outsiders happened to worship the "wrong deity." And this "deity" becomes a slippery slope because more people have been artificially killed and subjugated in the name of _a_ deity (whatever it is that they worshiped) than anything else in the world. For example, there have been natives who worshiped a volcano. And if you spoke ill about their religion, you would have gotten beaten-up to a pulp or massacred for _their_ version of blasphemy.

And you probably noticed that I keep coming full circle with religious beliefs. Why do you think is that? In simple terms, because religion is a catalyst for action. Religion tends to justify the unjustifiable if the followers are convinced enough of its merit. Most conflicts in human history can be directly traced to a religious justification for their actions. Want examples? Sure, here are a few from the top of my head in no particular order.

-Inquisition
-Genital Mutilation
-Civil Wars (to include the U.S. Civil War)
-Handling venomous snakes in a church service
-The crusades
-The Muslim religious wars between Shia and Sunni
-The massacre of Muslims in certain parts of South East Asia
-People refusing medical care to their children under religious grounds (resulting in the death of the children)
-The Holocaust
-Jim Crow laws

-Roe vs. Wade case in the supreme court about abortion
-All this *"political"* war against "woke"

I can go on, but I hope this makes the point. People tend to see the world from a very narrow lens. And for those who are not intellectually honest, whenever their world view is challenged then they will do all kinds of mental gymnastics to justify the unjustifiable. This is nothing new. It is part of human history, but at this point in our history we are supposed to be much better than where we are at now. History has repeated itself many times. The faces and flags might be different, but the tactics used by those who want to control the masses are very similar and proven effective. Why? Because we are more similar than different. That is why.

And it is ok if you realize that you too have been gullible or naïve. We all have at some point, it is ok. It is not how we fail, but how we recover that ultimately matters. Nobody is perfect, and we all have blind spots. Every one of us can make mistakes. If somebody claims they have made no mistakes, they are simply lying to you, and they are lying to themselves.

Not accepting that we are fallible is a logical fallacy on its own right. There is no such thing as perfection, and we all have room for improvement. Those who want to control you want you to believe that you have reached the apex of who you can be. And further they will use this to try to convince you that others outside your group are not "as smart as you," or worse that they are "inferior" because of whatever artificial reason they claim as empirical truth. It is a tactic as old as time itself, and it has been getting gullible people to do things that are against their best interests since forever.

Remember, for the authoritarian even the most loyal follower is disposable the moment this person becomes "inconvenient." We are seeing this today; it is clear as day for us who understand the links in history. It is not hard to discern if you understand this simple principle: When somebody poses an "us-against-them" narrative, it is likely because they are pushing propaganda. This propaganda in turn is benefiting a very narrow segment of the population. And counterintuitive as it might seem, the actual followers of this doctrine are not the ones who benefit from this narrative. They will be led to believe it does, but it does not.

Look at any authoritarian regime in history. Some of the closest followers might have been given a position of "power" but they also have to perpetually watch their backs. And those who were not very close to the top, but helped those move to the top are going to experience marginal improvements to their lives, or run the high risk of having their lives destroyed – even if they do not understand how or why.

Intellectual honesty is about introspection. You are more than welcome and have the right to become the person that you are meant to be. But you do not have the right to deny others from becoming the person *they* are meant to be. What you feel is good for *you* might not be what *they* consider right for *themselves*. The first question should be? Is what they are doing affecting you directly or by proxy? Does your life change in any <u>negative</u> way? And this change must be objective, not conjecture. Food for thought as we move to our last chapter.

CHAPTER 8

ARE YOU WOKE?|
Food for Thought

As we are arriving to this book's final chapter, what is your answer to this chapter's title? *By the time you've reached this chapter, we've covered a lot of compounding contexts in this book. You probably noticed than in the last chapters I did not repeatedly utter the word "woke." – but we spoke among other things a lot about being intellectually honest, and avoiding becoming useful fools or a target for an opportunistic "dear leader" overlord. Fun fact, a lot of people who can see above the propaganda horizon actually stated that "woke" is in-fact a good thing. Those who disagree after truly understanding the context tend to be demagogs, propagandists (charlatans), or useful fools who parrot divisive platitudes. That is why a lot of sabotage onto a "woke" mentality has been infiltrated by those I mentioned, and a number of others I did not specifically mentioned, but they do exist. Going back to the basics in this book -yet paraphrased for effect: "Woke" is a euphemism for being alert about not getting jammed in a bad situation up-society's behind. Somebody wins when segments of society fight among each other over a false narrative, or a faux-outrage. And as we discussed before, it is not every member of society, or even the supporters of the dissenters who win in this situation. In the end all useful fools are disposable whenever they are deemed inconvenient to the "dear leader." And remember, the topic of dissent is incidental at best. It is more about how exploitable is whatever bias you actually have, and how it can give leverage to their selfish agenda. So I ask you again, are you actually "woke?" Or are you dozed-off under a charlatan's propaganda?*

When I came with the title for this book, I knew that some people would have very mixed feelings and misconceptions about this topic – and indeed the very title is meant to be open-ended. Who are the charlatans? Whose inconvenience? Simple questions, complex answers. Short answer, it can be any one of us if we are vulnerable enough to fall for an opportunistic manufactured narrative. In fact, don't feel bad if you have indeed been a victim. It is part of learning. The question is: How can we independently recover from it?

Before you answer that question. Let us emphasize that it is easy falling for those traps. They are designed to be that way. Propaganda is a sinister art form. There are a lot of subtleties that will make it counter intuitive to even fight against it. But remember what I said, it is designed to be palatable, but when it is based on a falsehood the math is not going to add up somewhere. And this lack of integrity in the equation is inconvenient to the propagandist. Hence dissent will be demonized and attacked – but not on the actual merits of the situation.

We have seen it time and time again during world's history. It is nothing new, but the tactics will continue to improve based on the environment. For some people who are unfamiliar with these dynamic changes that have occurred over time, they will be more prone to become victims of these incendiary narratives. Simple enough, huh? Yes, but as you read in the pages before this chapter, the combinations and subtleties are very abstract and can go unnoticed to even some of the shrewdest observers… if they lose their intellectual honesty at some point. In other words, we can all become victims of our own biases.

The way you can raise above all this starts by understanding the actual merits of the issue in contention to any "controversy." Those merits are not necessarily what the pretty talking head in your device of choice is telling you. During the contention of these merits, a huge red flag is if the pretty talking head is talking derogatorily about a person – as in character assassination, rather than the actual merits for disagreement with *that* person. And yes, *that* person can be a natural air breathing human, or an artificial person such as a company.

If we are honest with ourselves, we can probably recall about at least a few times in our lives where we performed significant mental gymnastics in order to advocate in favor of a personal bias. Yes, long sentence. But in reality, we know that what I just said is part of human nature. We are all capable of getting a visceral sensation that just <u>feels</u> it is the right course of action – at the time. Much like when people get a crush on somebody, even if this crush does not come to fruition. But at *that* moment, there is this visceral response, you cannot simply run away from this feeling – even if you conceal it, and you either become hyper aware of your shortcomings or lose at least some control of your faculties. In a similar fashion, propaganda will find that bias and exploit it. That is why we can all become vulnerable to certain narratives.

However, this propensity will change as we live and learn. That is why intellectual honesty must always come hand-in-hand with critical thinking. Otherwise, critical thinking alone will just foster cynicism, and could even turn an otherwise good and decent person into a platitudes-parroting fool. For those who know what to look for, they can see the writing on the wall miles away and avoid it outright. For those who are not quite there yet, will either struggle to see the actual truth, or remain blinded to it. Sometimes willfully.

We are the product of our environment. Things that become normalized around us will tend to dictate our perception of our "reality." And in case you did not realize it by now, collective bias exploitation is very much an alternative for a propagandist. That is part of what is known as group thinking. Let me give you a mundane, yet benign example. Being part of the crowd in a stadium and people start doing "the wave." Most people tend to follow the crowd and play along with the fun. There is no rehearsal, no briefing, no asking for permission. The event becomes spontaneous, and people join in. And in this case, it can be very fun. It is very similar in concept for the propagandists but a lot more complex in execution. In other words, no matter how complex something gets, there will be some basic elements that can be identified. How these will be arranged will convey potentially an infinite number of possibilities.

Want an illustrative example? Sure, music. For most musical instruments there are only a certain number of notes in an octave (C, D, E, F, G, A, B and C), but based on how you arrange these notes you can have an incalculable number of combinations. We can argue that we can add a bit more complexity based on the full span of notes within an octave (C, C#, D, D#, E, F, F#, G, G#, A, A#, B and C). The more we end up combining those sounds, the more we can express exceedingly intricate levels of musical emotion. Moreover, a composition does not need to have "a lot" of notes in order to have a deep emotional connection with the listener. Proper dynamics and well-placed notes will be able to elicit a great range or emotions based on the musician's skill. Some music compositions will make you want to dance, others might make you cry, some might uplift you, some will inspire you, while others might doze you off…etc.

Propaganda is very much the same. It is going to bring a response and some sort of "connection" with our senses. That is why a lot of people who are being taken as useful fools will feel blinded to this reality. It is just counterintuitive to them because they are being deceived in a multidimensional manner. If you have been a victim of this, I said it before and I say it again. It is ok, propaganda is designed to do exactly that. It is hard for anybody to ask a question they did not know they were supposed to ask. That is why it is so effective. Especially if your loved ones are also victims of a similar narrative. It is not a black and white situation; it is a gigantic gradient.

When it comes to group thinking, there will always be "somebody else <u>out</u> of the core group." In other words, an "us against them" type narrative. Again, it is designed to be that way by somebody who has a vested interest in your reaction. Whatever this reaction might be. What does that mean? A reaction in favor of their narrative, or a dismissal if they already decided to put you in the opposite end of that dichotomy.

True that in some instances the propagandist will hit a lucky strike. If that happens, you can be sure they will capitalize on those coincidences. In fact, some of those propagandists might even be delusional enough to think that they are actually spot-on if a coincidence does occur. Yes, some people get convinced of their own bullshit story. Surprise!

In either case, if you have gained enough introspection and are able to raise above the falsehood and gaslighting, then you will realize that no matter what bullshit story people try to give you, there is a formula to figure out if it makes sense or not. And no, being spot-on and figuring out *something else* that was skewed at *some time* in your life does not necessarily mean that you'll automatically be immune to being naïve against something else in the future. Even a mathematician can make a mistake when attempting on resolving their equations from time to time. Some of these skills are quite perishable indeed. By the way, that is why we have peer review processes. However, if you keep your skills sharp by paying attention to what we've spoken in the previous chapters, your chances from getting bamboozled will diminish dramatically. It is up to you.

By now we discussed the dictionary, colloquial, and historical uses of this "woke" terminology. We also discussed how this word has been weaponized.

The fact is that "woke" being a term that got demonized is largely incidental and derivative for what it actually stands for. It could have been any other word that would advocate for fairness across the board. The result would have been the same demonization "woke" has achieved. Why? Because it is inconvenient to those who want to push a false narrative, that is why.

Don't worry, "woke" is not a demonic thing (as far as religiousness), however it is a target of opportunity to create division. Authoritarians have a very high vested interest in dividing people, no matter where in the world they thrive. Among other things it makes the authoritarian's job a lot easier when they are surrounded by useful fools who will cling onto their every platitude. This is not a left or right side of the political spectrum either. It is a "people" vulnerability based on our circumstances.

Again, and I keep repeating it for a reason. In the event you can identify in your lives' history an instance where you have been one of those useful fools, or one of those people parroting platitudes and propaganda talking points innocently, don't beat yourself up about it. You have a simple yet very powerful choice. Choose not to give any more power to those who used your candor and fervor in defense of a falsehood. There is a possibility that you are going to be hard on yourself. This whole realization might be traumatic in one way or the other to many people (if applicable). If that is you – don't worry. You will make it to the other side. Same way as million others had to deal with something similar in the past. Chances are that a lot of those were in your cross-hairs before you learned about these things, and you disagreed under the guise of a falsehood. They probably already had to deal with the same process you are going through right now.

If the realization of having been a victim of propaganda gets you mad, you're right to be upset. But don't let it consume you. I've said it before, I say it again. It is not how you fall, but rather how you recover that ultimately matters. YOU can make a difference to help others raise above the falsehoods. Just remember that if it was hard for you, it might be even harder for some others – depending how deep in their convictions they are now placed based on these falsehoods.

With this I am not advocating for you to become an activist or start a counter protest against those who lied to you (unless you want to, but that is your decision not mine). In order to win it is as easy as to deprive them from your undivided attention and devotion. The truth in the end will come to light. It might take years, might take centuries even, but facts are impervious to emotion. As I said before, when something is true it does not matter how complex it is, every piece will fall in place automatically. A falsehood will have parts that will not match up. That is not the same as a miscalculation, because even in a miscalculation there will be another empirical science that will be able to shed some light onto the discrepancy, and even demonstrate if there was a miscalculation elsewhere. And by combining all these data points we can reach a viable resolution.

When you stop and think about it, that is what this "woke" phenomenon is all about. It sheds light onto the darkness of what we have been accustomed to thrive upon. It opens your eyes to something that was perhaps just out of sight, but it very much existed all along. In other words "opening our eyes, as in being awake" and see reality for what it is.

What we perceive from first-hand perspective is not necessarily the entire story. And yes, part of the story line will be inconvenient if somebody is seeking to manipulate people under a falsehood. For propaganda to be effective, there has to be "some truth" intermingled somewhere between all the falsehoods, half-truths, and misdirection. But any information charlatans will give you will be cherry picked at best. They don't want you to have full context. It is not convenient for them. Even if they don't make it look obvious at all.

I mentioned before, if a propagandist would tell you ALL the truth about their misguided doctrines, they would likely not get any following. The only way they can get support is if they "redact" important facts that would derail their opposition's narrative on the merits. Instead they will resort to lies and cheating, or concealment of important information to prevent the proper context from reaching your objective judgment. In other words, they rig the game in an attempt to win. But winning a rigged game is in-fact losing, no matter what the scoreboard says. If you know that you won by cheating, it does not matter who you lie to (even if they believe you), you cannot lie to yourself. If you cheated, then you know that you were always the loser, because you never actually won. Even if you have a "trophy" and others celebrated your "deceitful" win. If you did not win fair and square, you lost.

Propagandists and authoritarians play that rigged game. They pose as the winners, but they know they are in-fact losers. That is why they can never "accept defeat" – or they act as though they "never make mistakes" – or they "are always right." That is the same reason why if there is any discrepancy "somebody else is at fault." They are never satisfied because they know that they are losers. And by extension they have very low self-esteem because of it, and will try to overcompensate for it. It is not that they are just trying to lie to you or whomever will listen, they are constantly lying to themselves.

Again, winning by cheating is a de-facto loss.

Are there people who tarnish the "woke" by chance or in a premeditated way? Absolutely yes. It is expected. It is a tactic to conduct character assassination. In other words, the authoritarian and propagandists are afraid, therefore they resort to cheating. It is clear as day when you know what you are seeing. It gets clearer the more you see the patterns, and the more you get acquainted with the examples.

Soon enough, you'll realize that those who are useful fools will constantly back up the wrong narrative. The patterns become ever so clear. They will always be on the wrong side of the battle. They might score some up-points every now and then, but they will eventually always lose.

I told you at the beginning of the book, if somebody calls me "woke" I don't take it as a personal insult. Under the factual definitions and context I have elaborated in this book, now you realize what it means - having critical thinking, intellectual honesty, and winning without cheating.

With this we have reached the end of this chapter. Ask yourself, knowing what you now know, are you also "woke?" You don't need to answer this question to me, the answer was inside you all along, even if you had to learn something new to put it into context. Thank you for taking the time to read my book and spending these moments with me! HLC

ACKNOWLEDGEMENTS

THANK YOU! First to all my readers! I appreciate so much that you are taking the time to read my words. I realize you could be reading or doing anything else, and you chose to read what I had to say. I appreciate that very much!

Thank you to my wife Alicia and my daughter Samantha for always being there for me, even if I am on the opposite side of the planet from time to time. Once again, like the very moment I am typing these words and the ship is underway somewhere in the Atlantic Ocean. As always, love has no bounds, and I love you both no matter if you are in my arms or halfway around the world, I love you all the same... I wish I was closer (especially as I write this).

Thank you to the crew of USS COLE DDG 67 during this [yet another] long time away from homeport. It is not a deployment, but it does feel insanely long ago since we've been home. Love you guys but I am happy that finally in a few days I'll be off the boat and spend time with my girls and enjoy the closest thing we can have for a mini-vacation... in a big American City. The Big Apple – New York City!

To whomever is it that will end up publishing and distributing this book. Which at the time I am writing this, I have no idea who it will be, not yet anyway... It will likely be myself via some outlet I have not yet decided or some book self-publishing house, as an E-book, audio book... or who knows? Once I know I will add the proper credit right below this paragraph (yes, I am keeping this paragraph, this is happening, let us live with it). And yes, we might see this same line in all my books. Because it remains true.

EPILOGUE

The manuscript for

WOKE & PROUD | The Charlatans' Inconvenience

is finally a tangible reality!

This is the fourth book I wrote, and finished – there are a few others in the works. I started writing this manuscript on Friday, March 17, 2023. So much has happened since then, and finally I am writing this epilogue on Sunday, May 21, 2023. An hour or so earlier I finished typing the last chapter for this book.

Ironically, this is the shortest manuscript I've written thus far – and it almost feels like it is the one that took the longest. In reality I was doing pretty good time at first but then for the last few chapters took me a long time to re-engage. It was a bit frustrating because I knew exactly what I wanted to type. I just did not have the time to do so. That's the Navy life for you.

For the last several weeks we've been away from home. It has been extremely busy and taxing. Finally, as I completed most of the pressing issues, I decided to use some of my scarce down-time to finish writing what was on my mind. It actually took me so long to re-engage on this manuscript that I even had to proof-read chapters one thru seven, finish chapter seven, and type the last chapter yesterday and today. The good news is that this book should not take too long to read, but I am happy with the message contained herein. However, as I sit here, I have no idea how long it will take to make it available to you all.

Also yes, there is some strategic redundancy in this book, but it was designed to be that way in order to reinforce some key points. I am well aware those important points needed repetition to reaffirm the context as the chapters moved forward.

With that said, as previously mentioned the book is intended to be a short reading. The reason is because the topic is emergent, therefore I wanted to drive the message as quickly as possible. However, I was not going to sacrifice exactitude for the sake of brevity. Whenever I have that option, that is the option I will take. I rather invest time to save time (yes, that is actually a thing). It might be counterintuitive for some people, but it has worked well in my life. Now, as I am laying down in my bunk for the night, I just want to bask on the realization that this is the fourth manuscript I've finished typing onboard this world-famous warship – the mighty USS COLE DDG 67.

Much like the other books I've written, I am in a weird typing position. I don't have enough room to sit up. Therefore I have my trusty Microsoft Surface Pro tablet & keyboard propped over my left leg as my left foot is resting on my right foot, which is also in a weird angle. And yes, that's the most comfortable position I could find. My keyboard is resting on my belly just a couple of inches below my belly button. Other parts of my book I was able to type in the Mess Decks and the Chiefs Mess onboard USS COLE. However all those places tend to get noisy and it is distracting. Here it is the end of the night and it is possibly the closest thing to privacy I can find. Also, in most places I work onboard we cannot bring personal electronic devices as matter of doctrinal regulations.

Part of this book was also written while at home. This was mostly when my daughter was enjoying her shows on TV and I was making her company. It is nice being together, I got to see her have some fun while we hang out together doing our own thing. Of course, after she was done with her TV shows, we would go out and have fun, running errands, going for dinner, shopping, or any of our usual activities. Sammy is my little buddy, and I am so lucky to be her dad. And yes, the book took a back seat if my daughter wanted to spend time with me.

By the time this book is out, perhaps one of my previous manuscripts will already be published. This book is sort of a spin-off from the previous one. In other words the topics I'm writing about in each manuscript are related, but each is an important topic on its own right. Hence my need to dedicate a book to this subject (as well as the other subjects). That way this book can be read stand-alone, or compliment the context with my other book(s). And when it comes to my writing, that is exactly what I want to do. I want to ensure my books are linked in relevant juncture points.

The truth is that there is always so much in my mind. And putting everything in one book would be impossible. That is why the other manuscripts I've written will be released in a manner that compliments this book theme. Also, that gives me time to work through the publishing process. I've decided to try the self-publishing route and leverage my small multimedia company [BeeZee Vision, LLC] to that end.

It just makes sense to me. Afterall, these are my books, these are my words, and the way I visualize things is very particular. Quite frankly, I don't want to be subject to the whims of somebody who might or might not have a negative bias about my writing content. It is liberating, because whatever the case I am keeping control of my message (and my words) once it make its way into the world without it being editorialized.

And let me tell you. It has been quite a learning experience. Writing the manuscripts is one thing, but making it available to the world is quite a different beast. But I am ready for the challenge. If you're reading these words, it is because I figured it out, and whatever is it that I did work as intended. Yeah! Thank you for reading my words. Again, I know you could be reading anything else but you chose to spend this time with me. I am grateful and appreciate you very much!

ABOUT THE BOOK

"Woke" is one of the most misunderstood words in the modern English vernacular. The character assassination to this term can easily be linked to propagandistic attempts by authoritarians, and authoritarians wanna-be. The term "woke" seem to be hijacked by opportunists and defined in ways that defy coherence.   In this book we get to define the term, understand its historical use, and how this *faux controversy* contributes to propagandists and other unsavory charlatans' narratives. Many will find this short read full of mind-blowing facts. Regardless of how you currently feel about "woke" - everybody should be able to appreciate the clarification process. We are just speaking demonstrable facts in these pages. In the end you will get to define "woke" for what really it is. And most importantly you will be able to know the answer to the question: Is the reader of this book actually "woke?" Find out, the answer might surprise you.

ABOUT THE AUTHOR

J. Marcelo Baqueroalvarez was born in San Francisco de Quito, Republic of Ecuador. After moving to the United States in 1995, he enrolled and graduated Fort Lauderdale High School and subsequently college at the Art Institute of Fort Lauderdale with Magna Cum Laude in 1999. Simultaneously, he worked in video production and multimedia with his family until 2003 when he enlisted in the United States Navy. During his tenure in uniform, he traveled the world and was stationed at several commands, including USS SEATTLE (AOE-3), USS LAKE ERIE (CG-70), USS ABRAHAM LINCOLN (CVN-72), USS COLE (DDG-67) and additional commands on shore and overseas. He rose to the rank of Senior Chief Petty Officer. During his time in the Navy, he met his wife, Alicia, and they welcomed to the world their daughter, Samantha. Marcelo is an avid lover of the arts, particularly in music, graphic art, photography, videography, and writing. He uses his unique leadership style to nurture his peers, subordinates, and seniors, hoping to inspire and bring team cohesion. In 2013, he founded BeeZee Vision, LLC™ as an opportunity to expand his artistic acumen. He also started the Half Life Crisis™ project where he shares his unique points of view for posterity, doing what he loves the most which is stating facts.

ABOUT HALF LIFE CRISIS™

Half Life Crisis™ is the brainchild of J. Marcelo "BeeZee" Baqueroalvarez.

The simple concept is complex in execution. Half Life Crisis™ is not synonym with "midlife crisis." Half Life Crisis™ is the fact that we spend most of our lives making a living rather than living our lives. The project was designed as a catalyst to give his creator an avenue to do what he loves most. Which is to "rant," a lot, about all kinds of things he finds interesting or fascinating. During these "rants" he tells facts with exuberant detail. He has his say via the many media manifestations under the Half Life Crisis™ construct. Afterall, that is the entire reason Half Life Crisis™ was conceived in the first place. The project is aimed to be of interest to any person who is familiar with the concept of "adulting" – under the pragmatic understanding that not everybody who circled the sun 18 times or more actually qualifies as a functional adult. Half Life Crisis™ celebrates all those who have earned their "adulthood" even if they are under 18 years of age.

Because life is what we make of it...

www.halflifecrisis.com

ABOUT BeeZee VISION, LLC™

BeeZee Vision, LLC™ was founded on July 15, 2013, in the city of Chesapeake, Virginia, USA by J. Marcelo "BeeZee" Baqueroalvarez. The original idea from BeeZee Vision started in early 2005. BeeZee Vision, LLC™ is the brainchild of J. Marcelo Baqueroalvarez, and the company was founded along with his brother David R. Baquero as a web-development and multimedia company in 2003. The company supplies fully customized and automated professional web development services, as well as various selected multimedia services. The name BeeZee Vision comes from Marcelo's U.S. Navy nickname "BeeZee," which derives from his last name Baqueroalvarez, which in Navy jargon it means "Well Done." Creating professional and artistically inspired multimedia projects are Marcelo's personal vision and commitment.

BeeZee Vision, LLC™ serves as the multimedia vehicle for Marcelo's Half Life Crisis™ project. These books are the first iteration of BeeZee Vision, LLC™ embarking in publishing written material from concept to completion.

www.beezeevision.com

www. BZVweb.com

PUBLISHING ADMIN AND RIGHTS

This entire book was written by J. Marcelo Baqueroalvarez. There are no co-authors, though his wife Alicia D. Baqueroalvarez at some point offered to be the preliminary editor. Afterall, English is Marcelo's third language, so one day… sometime… he plans on learning how to speak proper English. Today is not that day, tomorrow does not look good either. There is a non-zero chance Alicia changed her mind, and this book was likely professionally edited at some point. Possibly by Marcelo Baqueroalvarez himself using Artificial Intelligence software. Hey, modern problems require modern solutions, right?

The book was mostly written onboard USS COLE DDG-67 during the very sporadic times in homeport at Norfolk, Virginia, and while spending lot of time underway somewhere in the Atlantic Ocean, and while the ship was tied to a pier in a few places along the Eastern Atlantic. And by a lot of days it means an insane number of days out to sea, and away from homeport.

The entire book's manuscript was typed in his Microsoft Surface Pro tablet/laptop, in Microsoft Word. Seriously, even the layout and fonts were done in the same laptop… on his lap, while he was laying after the workday… in his sleeping quarters, or in one of the mess halls onboard the ship.

This book and its contents are the intellectual property of J. Marcelo Baqueroalvarez, and distributed under Half Life Crisis™ and BeeZee Vision, LLC™, both also owned by J. Marcelo Baqueroalvarez. The rights of this book extend to his wife Alicia D. Baqueroalvarez and daughter Samantha B. Baqueroalvarez… and that is it. If there are any other publishing houses, then we will talk business then. But this manuscript was typed only by Marcelo. Alicia and Samantha Baqueroalvarez also own the rights for this book and all its derivates. It will remain so, unless officially noted otherwise. That has not happened yet, the book is likely going to be self-published. But ideally, we'll have follow-on editions and translate it in different languages. We'll see, stranger things have happened before.

COVER DESIGN RIGHTS & CONCEPT

© J Marcelo Baqueroalvarez | HLC 2023.

The original book cover design for "**WOKE & PROUD | The Charlatans' Inconvenience**" was conceptualized, designed, and created by J. Marcelo Baqueroalvarez. The inspiration for the cover design was derived from a paining from his daughter Samantha B. Baqueroalvarez

The original painting for the background image in this book cover's design was created by Samantha B. Baqueroalvarez.

This original painting is titled "**Turbulence**" and is of 1 of 3 pieces in her "**Beautiful Chaos**" collection. This original painting in particular was completed on March 15, 2021 using acrylic over an 8"x10" stretched canvas.

For the book cover inspiration, and adaptation, this painting from my daughter Samantha encapsulated the symbology that I wanted to convey. What I saw is an orange-red-colored figure who is laying down, seems to be awakening from a slumber while below this figure, another purple-colored figure remains asleep surrounded by darkness. The awaken figure is facing a green layered current with big pools of clarity at its core.

Below this complex current there is a layer darkness with flashes of orange light. There is a single green arch that links a path from the darkness to a small speck of clarity. This clarity is linked through a narrow path to a bright orange and yellow dichotomy. A similar color dichotomy that is represented in the awakened figure, although the figure has an orange-red and yellow dichotomy that is a bit darker than the top of the painting.

The yellow represent our enlightened pure essence; the altruistic good nature that supposed to exists in all of us. There yellow is also at the feet of the awakening figure because being good is the base for who we are. Even if sometimes the good in us is neglected. The brighter yellow up above in the image is the pure essence of the collective of those who understand right from wrong. The orange represents our learning process.

The figure also has a lot of orange-red representing our intrinsic fears and anxieties mixed with our learning process while being challenged in our world-view, much like our continuous attempt to fit in with the rest of the world as we are pushed outside our comfort zone. The bright orange up-above clears the red-anxiety and turns into self- acceptance of the collective helping us ascend to that pure essence.

In the darkness we see some specks of orange, symbolizing the fact that there is good and knowledge even when misinformation and propaganda tries to opaque the light. Below the purple figure slumbers in the darkness, ignoring the little bit of orange wisdom that is available. The only way the slumbered figure can reach that wisdom is by turning around and prescind their willful ignorance.

As the awaken figure looks up, the darkness behind the lessons stays further away from sight, and the wisdom and the pure essence dichotomy come closer to the figure's gaze.

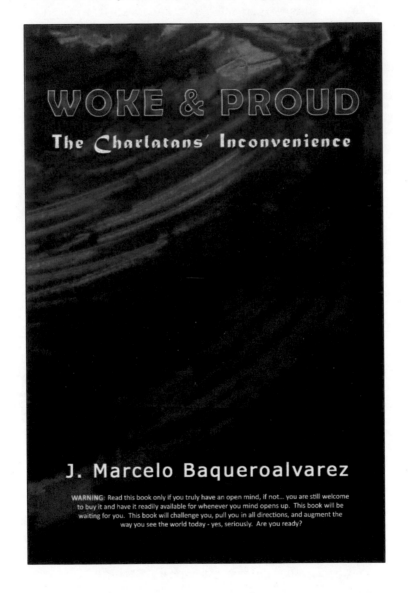

This image spoke to me as it summarizes in some manner the awakening complexity I want to convey with this book.

For official copies and written permission regarding this book, its derivatives and other original pieces from this author please contact the author via his official website as listed below:

www.halflifecrisis.com

WWW.HALFLIFECRISIS.COM

HALF LIFE CRISIS™

Because life is what we make of it...